CW01084488

THIRTY-FIVE ACRES,

A SPADE AND A FORK

THIRTY-FIVE ACRES, A SPADE AND A FORK

Kathleen Fleming

Copyright © 2013 by Kathleen Fleming.

ISBN: Softcover   978-1-4931-4425-9
              Ebook   978-1-4931-4426-6

All rights reserved. No part of this book may be reproduced or transmitted in any form or by any means, electronic or mechanical, including photocopying, recording, or by any information storage and retrieval system, without permission in writing from the copyright owner.

This book was printed in the United States of America.

Rev. date: 11/26/2013

To order additional copies of this book, contact:
Xlibris LLC
0-800-056-3182
www.xlibrispublishing.co.uk
Orders@xlibrispublishing.co.uk
521372

CONTENTS

PART THREE: FURZE FARM, LINCOLNSHIRE

INTRODUCTION

This book has three sections: 'Seven Years and Seven Landladies', 'Hobbs Hayes Farm', and 'Furze Farm'.

The seven landladies all have fictitious names except for the last, Mrs Isan, who was killed fairly recently, crossing the road opposite the Catholic church, coming home from church. The school was next door to the church, and for at least ten years, we had been badgering for a pedestrian crossing opposite to the Nuneaton to Coventry road. Both the headmaster and the parish priest had also been asking for this privilege, but it was declined, until she was killed. Since then they have put a crossing there.

I would like this book to be in memory of Mrs Isan.

PART ONE

SEVEN YEARS AND SEVEN LANDLADIES

No. 1 MRS ARMITAGE

In May 1949, I suddenly realised that the time had come to start looking for a job in September. I chose Warwickshire as the county in which I wished to teach because it is adjacent to Worcestershire. My parents lived in Dudley, where my father was a Church of England curate, and I hoped to be near them without being expected to live at home. In my anxiety over my interview, I confused morning—and afternoon-train times and arrived hot and bothered and late. However, I did get the job, and I was posted to Ansley Common, which is on a colliery estate.

I got lodgings with Mrs Armitage, a widow who was having difficulty making ends meet. As I would not get my twenty-nine-pound net pay until the end of the month, my father lent me twenty pounds for expenses.

The estate was a typical tight-knit community, and I did not have the social skills to make myself at home there. I was very much 'the teacher', an outsider who had to be respected, and an awkward silence always thwarted any attempt I made to socialise. My landlady, too, treated me very professionally, only speaking to me on business matters. The only relief I had from work was the occasional game of badminton with my colleagues in the school hall after the children had gone home. I looked forward to the weekends, when I went home and retired to my own den in the attic, where I had stencilled ships of my own design around the walls.

It was coming up—my twenty-first birthday. I had been on the estate for nearly a year but had not got to know anyone well enough to ask them to celebrate my birthday with me, so I decided to treat my parents to an orchestral concert in Birmingham. One of the items was a Beethoven symphony, which I knew they would particularly enjoy. That morning, I received a letter from my father. In it, he said that as it was my twenty-first, he would forget the twenty pounds I owed him. I had forgotten it long ago!

Straight after school, I went to Birmingham. Only my mother was there to meet me. I asked where my father was, and she answered, 'Oh, the vicar's mother called a meeting which he thought he ought to go to.' I was deeply hurt. Not even the vicar but the vicar's mother! I struggled to stifle my tears throughout the overture.

At school, an elderly teacher took the reception class. She must have been well past retiring age, and we called her Auntie. She was very good to me and mothered me. She had a nephew, David. She must have thought I would be a suitable partner for him as she made several attempts to get us together, but neither of us was interested. Eventually, she arranged for us to meet for a game of tennis, and we had an enjoyable game. Afterwards, we had a polite afternoon tea with Auntie and then said farewell. We never met again!

I was well into my second year at Ansley. One evening while preparing work for school, I sat back into my chair to consider my next step when the house seemed to give a little shudder, and my pen rolled off the table. I trembled and thought, *It's time I got out of this dump.* I picked up my pen, packed up my work, and went downstairs to make a cup of cocoa. I met Mrs Armitage in the hall. She looked distraught and said, 'I hope there hasn't been an accident in the pit!'

I had forgotten about the incident and felt ashamed of myself as I had been living on the colliery estate for nearly two years and hadn't given a thought to the mine. No wonder I hadn't been accepted into the community! I looked out of the window before going to bed and saw several groups of folk talking in the street.

Next morning, everyone was full of the news. No, there had not been a mining accident, but there had been a minor earthquake. The headmaster was very upset because quite a valuable vase had slithered off his mantelpiece. We would probably have known nothing about the tremor if it hadn't been for the mine workings underneath the houses.

I had the offer of a post at the Roman Catholic school in Nuneaton come September, and I would be starting a new life in the town.

No. 2 MR AND MRS BAILEY

After some searching, I found some digs near the centre of the town which would be more handy for anything that was going on, although there was precious little so soon after the war.

Mr and Mrs Bailey were newly-weds, living in a neat little semi-detached house in a quiet street. Mrs Bailey, Belinda, was a pretty little butterfly of a thing, very proud of her new furniture, which I suspected was bought on tick—no doubt the reason I was intruding on their love nest!

Mr Bailey, a schoolteacher with upper juniors, was much more down to earth. Every night, he would come home with piles of maths books to mark during tea. He and I would pore over a child's book now and again to try to decipher why he or she had every sum wrong. Was there a basic misunderstanding somewhere? He also told me about a play he was producing at the Methodist church at the end of the road. The action of which was supposed to be taking place on a boat sailing down a canal.

One Friday night, he came home most distressed. 'The chappie painting the scenery has no idea of perspective,' he said. 'The canal is supposed to disappear into the distance.'

'I could help you with that,' I said enthusiastically. 'That's if I wouldn't be treading on anybody's toes.' We arranged to go down to the chapel together on Monday night.

We left the house just before seven to walk a few yards down the road. The painting on the backcloth was a shambles, but fortunately, everybody seemed relieved that I had come along and was quite happy for me to completely revamp it. I got into it straight away, ignoring the action going on below me. I wasn't particularly relaxed painting while up a ladder. Only at the finale did I take notice of my surroundings. On either side towards the back of the stage were capstans with a clothes horse behind each. These had puzzled me. Then, the principal boy released the rope from the capstan and dramatically threw it over the clothes horse as we heard the engines starting up. He kissed his girl centre stage as they were to sail away to live happily ever after. To my horror, I realised that the clothes horses were the ship's rails, which I had to continue painting around the foredeck.

By ten o'clock, we were both shattered and walked back to the little doll's house in silence. I went straight to bed. We continued the next night and for the rest of the week. He, with tutoring different groups, and I was beginning to really enjoy painting my Dutch canal scene. By the end of the second week, I had blocked in houses on both sides with brightly coloured bulb fields beyond. I had charcoaled in the windows and doors and, with difficulty, the ship's rails. I would finish it well before the end of the next week.

I wanted to go home on Friday evening.

On Saturday morning, Mr Bailey was already at breakfast when I handed Belinda my rent.

'Go!' she said.

'Where?' I asked.

'I don't know, just go.'

'If you don't want me here, give me a chance to find somewhere else.'

'Go now!' she demanded.

I looked over to Mr Bailey. He shrugged his shoulders. I went upstairs, packed my case, and gathered up the schoolwork I had planned to do over the weekend.

When I came down, Mr Bailey was reading the paper. I tapped him on the shoulder and said, 'I think I've done enough for someone else to finish.' He nodded without raising his head.

'Go,' she shouted from the kitchen. I left without further ceremony.

First, I went to the school. It was closed, so I hid my school materials in the parish hall, which was open for a Brownie session. I then sat in the park, wondering what to do next. I could have kicked myself for not realising what our evening pilgrimages down to the chapel must have looked like to Belinda, let alone huddling over kids' maths books together. And I couldn't even remember his Christian name!

I decided I had only one option—get on a bus to Coventry, find the YMCA, and see if I could get a bed for the night there.

Yes, they came to my rescue. I was shown a bed in a room more like an old-fashioned hospital ward than a bedroom. My only privacy was a locker at the side of my bed. It was lucky I only had a suitcase of belongings. I had never felt quite so lonely. I wandered around Coventry for a bit, then bought a packet of blank postcards, and painted one or two sketches of the old town. After traipsing around to find somewhere suitable to eat, I did some more sightseeing. I wearily went back to the hostel and straight to bed. Soon the dormitory began to fill up. The girls on either side of me talked excitedly across me as if I wasn't there. I wouldn't have known what to talk about if I had been brought into the chatter as I had no glamorous heart-throb to boast about . . . . Mr Bailey? No never! I was glad the warden was strict about lights out, although this made precious little difference to the noise level.

Roll on, Monday! I thought the six-year-old children in my class much better company.

No. 3 CONNIE

All the following week, I tried desperately to find new digs and fled home immediately after school on Friday. I didn't have any luck on the next week either. When I passed the Methodist chapel, I looked ruefully at the poster advertising *Romance on the Canal*. I would have dearly liked to have known how the backcloth looked in the fully dressed production, but no way could I go in. During the third week, I finally found a place to stay and arranged to move in on the Sunday.

My step quickened as I approached Connie's house. It had been built between the wars, a detached corner house with large bay windows and on a slight rise. The small front garden was neat, just a lawn and a paved path to the front door. Connie greeted me politely in a high-pitched monotone voice. She was not far short of forty, with dark hair scraped back with a comb. Slight in build and with a colourless complexion, she was dressed in dark brown.

She showed me into the dining room, which was dark, with heavily embossed wallpaper and brown paintwork. She then took me to my bedroom. This had similar decor. I was puzzled as to how a house that appeared so open from the outside could be so claustrophobic inside. I made the best of my accommodation by moving the table to the window, but I thought, *Never had I met such a nondescript person living in such a nondescript house.*

I had lost my den at home too. My father was now a priest in charge of Ronkswood housing estate in Worcester, so my parents were living in a three-bedroomed council house. Father had the small bedroom as a study, and Mother had said, 'We must keep all this large furniture for when we get a vicarage.' It was stored in the spare bedroom, so I had to clamber over stacked furniture to get to bed.

I decided I must make some effort to socialise, so I joined the local music club. However, I was very shy and could not cope in a group of people who already knew each other. I resigned after a few meetings.

I had had a fascination for the Roman Catholic church since my school days. Although I felt some of the sentimental worship of Our Lady unpalatable, I thought it was now time to join the fold and went for formal instruction. My parents had always been very upset by my Roman Catholic leanings, but I persuaded myself that I was right to follow my conscience.

I was duly received and, shortly afterwards, invited to join the Legion of Mary. We met once a week for our devotions and a homily and were then assigned certain needy parishioners to visit in pairs. This proved to be the answer to my social problems. Whereas I had found it so difficult to integrate into a group of people, I enjoyed the company of a 'brother' or a 'sister' on a one-to-one basis when we went visiting.

I was particularly friendly with one of the sisters called Shelagh. Her fiancé was in an isolation hospital, suffering from TB, and when we went out for walks together, she always put me on the outside of the pavement; she was so used to going out with Alan. One of the brothers, Peter, asked me back to his house sometimes after church on a Sunday evening. I was spending fewer and fewer evenings in my dismal digs, and on the odd night I did stay in, I had so much schoolwork to catch up on that my surroundings didn't bother me. I noticed that Connie was spending more evenings out too and often got back after me, but I thought nothing of it. Then, in her high, flat tone, she made an announcement.

'I'm getting married!'

'Oh!' I said. I ought to have congratulated her there and then, but I was dumbfounded. *Well every man has his taste*, I thought.

'I'm afraid you will have to find other accommodation before the month is up.'

I thanked her for giving me generous notice and congratulated her.

I found new digs within a fortnight.

No. 4 MISS BROOKLEY

Miss Brookley lived in a bungalow situated in a mature garden. I hurried up to the front door. Miss Brookley was very welcoming—a tall woman getting on in years with almost white hair combed back into a bun. She had a red complexion and very light blue eyes.

There was plenty of glass in the house. Every window had a view of the rather unkempt garden. The walls were well furnished with pictures, mostly scenic. My room seemed pleasant enough, and she said to me, 'Feel free to move around the house. You may use the bathroom whenever you want, but I do make one stipulation. I always have a bath on a Friday night, and the hot-water tank will only fill one bath a night, so please make sure you never use the bathwater on a Friday night.'

I promised never to use any hot water on a Friday night and soon settled in. Most evenings, she was out, but when we did get together, we talked about everything from the atomic bomb to the life cycle of the dragonfly.

I was asked if I would take over the church cub pack. Reluctantly I agreed, but I thought being Akela for a pack of cubs every Wednesday after a day's teaching was a bit much. However, I enjoyed the challenge, and the scout jamborees at Warwick were superb. But I desperately needed an assistant. The parish priest said that an exceptional scout who was a devout Catholic had moved into the parish and was keen to help. I was delighted, and he arranged for us to meet after the eleven-o'clock mass the next Sunday.

At that mass, I couldn't help noticing a chap just in front of me who seemed a complete stranger. He had no notion when to sit or stand or act appropriately. This person turned out to be my proposed assistant. He came to the meeting the following Wednesday. He was full of grand ideas but didn't seem familiar with scout routine.

Micheal, one of the cubs, was subject to epileptic fits. He had never had one at a meeting, but I met him in town one Saturday, carrying a load of greengrocery. He was on his way to the bus station and then blacked out in the middle of the road just where the buses turned to the high street. Bus drivers were hooting and swearing at him, but he was unaware. When he came to, he had no idea what had happened, and various people helped him pick up his apples, which had rolled all over the road. This worried me as he had to cross this road to get home after cubs. When I found that my assistant lived in that direction, I asked him to see Micheal as far as the bus station.

I was feeling rather uneasy because what I had been told about this man did not match up to his behaviour. I decided to find out if the scouting authorities knew anything about him. They told me he had been blacklisted for abusing young boys. I was unbelievably relieved to see Micheal turn up unperturbed at the next cub meeting.

I would have liked to have taken over some of the cubs' camping but knew that I couldn't without the help of an experienced scout. I thought a day's ramble would be feasible if I were accompanied by a responsible adult. Peter volunteered. We arranged to go on the Friday which began the autumn half-term. I chose a footpath walk, which was very poorly defined and proved to be a good map-reading exercise. At one point, there was a stile and culvert over a ditch, but all was covered by a vast tangle of brambles and stinging nettles. We walked along the ditch to find a better place to cross. Peter jumped over, and I straddled the ditch to help the pack over. All made it quite easily except for one very overweight cub who had waited until last. Peter hauled him up to safety, but I lost my footing and slipped into the ditch. I laughed along with everybody else, but I was very muddy and decidedly damp.

We arrived back very tired, but exhilarated. Most of the cubs went home on their own, but a few were being met. All the parents were there except for Fatty's. Peter said he would wait, but as he was an unofficial helper, I felt obliged to stay. He had got mucked up too, so he went home. I waited and waited, but nobody turned up. I was just thinking about walking home with this child when a very apologetic dad turned up, saying he had been held up at work and missed the train at Birmingham.

I hurried back to Miss Brookley's, stripped off my dirty clothes, and jumped into the bath. I was enjoying a hot soak when I remembered it was Friday. I quickly got out, as if that would make any difference, and thought, *It's quite early still, maybe the water will heat up before she comes in.*

As soon as I got to bed, I went to sleep, but I was woken up by the door slamming and then another one. I lay awakened, then heard a third door slam. It was a long time before I got to sleep again.

In the morning, I wondered whether to sneak off home and give Miss Brookley time to cool off or apologise. I liked living here, so I decided to confront her. I went to the kitchen with trepidation.

'You took my bathwater,' she shouted.

'I . . .'

'You stole my bathwater!'

'I'm sorry . . .'

'Sorry my foot! I've made you quite at home here, and you abuse it.'

'I promise I will never do it again.'

'You can go.'

'I won't forget . . .'

'You won't have a chance to forget, you are going now!'

I was about to point out that we had agreed on a week's notice either way, but the red from her complexion had spread to the tips of her ears, and her blue eyes were flashing with rage. She would only have had to lift the toasting fork off the wall behind her, and she would have looked like the devil incarnate.

She turned her back on me, took down the toasting fork, and opened the fire door to make toast. She picked up the bread knife to cut the bread and then caught sight of me still standing in the doorway. She advanced towards me with the toasting fork in one hand and the bread knife in the other.

'*Go now.*'

Suddenly I didn't want to live here any more. I packed up my belongings, left the rent on the dressing table, and fled.

School didn't start again until Wednesday, so I returned home via Coventry, booking Tuesday night at the YMCA on the way.

No. 5 MRS BROWN

I had been three weeks at Coventry YMCA before I found accommodation with Mrs Brown. I had arranged to install myself there on the Sunday evening after spending the weekend at home with my parents. My father had now got a living as vicar of Himbleton and Huddington in Worcestershire. The nearest railway station was Droitwich, which was a six-mile walk from the vicarage. To get back to Nuneaton, I also had to change at Birmingham and sprint from Snowhill to New Street station. I often dozed on the train but usually woke up in Stockingford tunnel, which warned me that we would soon be pulling into Nuneaton station. However, on this occasion, I went fast asleep until we arrived at Coventry, where the train terminated. I asked when the next train back to Nuneaton would be, but it wasn't until the morning. In no way was I going to spend another night at the YMCA even if there had been a bed at that time of night. The weather was very mild for that time of year, so I decided to bed down on a bench in the station. There was a lot of traffic passing through and shunting going on all the time, but I got some sleep.

In the wee small hours of the morning, the stationmaster brought me a horribly sweet mug of tea, but it was piping hot and very welcome. I arrived at school on Monday morning rather dishevelled but soon forgot the night's experience when the children came in, bursting with enthusiasm for the latest class project.

Because she had no telephone, I had been unable to let Mrs Brown know that I would not be arriving on the Sunday evening. After school on Monday, I presented myself on her doorstep with great trepidation. Hers was a little terraced house with lace curtains, in the older part of Nuneaton. I hesitated and then knocked.

Mrs Brown was very welcoming. She made me a cup of tea while I explained what had happened. I forgot to say that I did not like sugar in my tea! Then she showed me to my room, which was at the back of the house and very small, but adequate. It overlooked the outhouses and a small backyard. This backed on to the backyards of the neighbouring street. The outbuildings housed the wash house, coal shed, and toilet. Besides the bed, I was provided with a bedside table, a chair, and a wash-hand stand. On this were the bowl and jug and also a soap bowl and a vase for toothbrushes. Underneath was the chamber pot, all decorated with a matching and very florid pink flower pattern.

Mrs Brown was quite elderly but kept the house beautifully. She was a short lady, of stocky build, with tightly permed grey hair. She had been in service all her life. She walked with a wobble and amused me because all the time she was at home she kept a spotless apron around her backside. Whenever anyone came to the door, she would whip it around to the front in case she had soiled her skirt in any way.

In spite of the cramped living conditions, I should have been quite content there. Mrs Brown was such a homely person. But with the trauma of Miss Brookley going berserk, the YMCA, where I felt like a fish out of water, and to say nothing of a night on Coventry station, I craved for some stability in my life.

It occurred to me that I might find that in a convent. I was totally committed to the faith at that time. I visited a teaching order with the vague idea that I might join the nuns at some time. The convent and classrooms were light and airy; everything was very well appointed, but even during that one afternoon, I felt boxed in as if I were being squeezed into a mould that did not fit. It was a day school, so the children were not there, but it seemed that the nuns were endeavouring to fit their pupils all into identical moulds too. I came away confused and disconcerted. On the Sunday, I went for a long walk in the country, relishing the open sky.

Anyway, I enjoyed going up to Peter's house on a Sunday evening, and we did go for the occasional day out together as well as visiting his sister, Barbara. Peter was a handsome young man of average height with fair hair and hazel eyes. He spoke very correctly, but with a slightly laboured dialect as if he had been subjected to many elocution lessons. This was probably true as his parents had owned a fish-and-chip business, and he had been born above the shop, something of which his mother was not proud!

We had a new member from Ireland join the Legion of Mary. His name was John Fleming, but he liked to be called Sean to underline his Irishness, although he needn't have bothered as he spoke with a very broad accent. He talked continuously about his 500 cc Norton motorbike although none of us were the slightest bit interested except the assistant parish priest who was our chaplain. Sean was dark-haired, had a high complexion, and wore strong glasses. He had very powerful shoulders and seemed like one with his big bike of which he was so proud. When I was on Legion work with him, I learnt that he loved farming and still owned some pigs in Ireland. He had advertised for a farm job over here because the pay was better, but he hoped to be able to buy his own land in Ireland in due course. Of the thirty replies to his advert, he had chosen the farm near Nuneaton because the pay was more, although the job did involve delivering the farm bottled milk as well.

Our latest new member in the Legion was a young girl called Betsie. She had curly auburn hair and freckles. Betsie was head over heels in love with Peter, literally. One day, when I asked her back to my room, she somersaulted on the bed in her exuberance. I was surprised how resentful I felt of her being in love with my Peter! I had never thought of him as 'my Peter' before. I was not jealous. She worked at the clothing factory where Peter was a manager, and he regarded her as a silly little teenager who had a crush on him and caused him considerable embarrassment in his job.

Peter was now president of the Legion of Mary in our parish and, as such, was responsible for pairing us up for our various visits. Betsie had joined the Legion, hoping she would be asked to make her visits along with her idol. Peter kept us in a more or less strict rota, but he never put himself on with Betsie. I went several times with her and listened patiently to her ramblings about her wonderful 'film-star' hero who said very little. She thought it was her freckles causing the problem. I assured her that it wasn't and added quite honestly 'They make you look even more attractive', but I added 'Peter is very reserved, you know.'

After three or four months of her unsuccessful romance, she got a new job in Coventry. She asked me if I knew of anywhere she could stay. I suggested the YMCA. I was sure she would feel much more at home there than I had ever done. Neither Peter nor any of the rest of us ever heard from her again.

A previous member of our legion was John Dewis. He came from Sedgley, where I had attended mass a few times when my parents lived at Dudley. He was a gentle, quietly spoken young man, quite good-looking but not stunningly handsome like Peter. He had left to go to the Beda College in Rome, where he was studying for the priesthood. He invited Peter over to Rome for a holiday the coming spring to see the sights. Peter asked me if I would like to come with him. I jumped at the idea, although I didn't know where I was going to get the money from. The airfare alone of £35 10s. 0d. was practically a month's salary. We talked about our plans at the next Legion meeting. Sean and Eileen said they would like to come too, so we arranged to go as a foursome.

Eileen was a colleague of mine at school. Although best of friends in the Legion, there was friction between us as class teachers. She was convent-trained, and both her aims and methods were different from mine. On occasions I lost my temper, and once I slapped her across the face. This was most unprofessional, and I had to suffer for it by eating humble pie.

None of this would colour our trip to Rome in the slightest as we were certainly not going to discuss the philosophy of teaching while in Rome!

Eileen was a pretty girl, and Sean was very taken with her. Her hair was naturally blonde and curly; she had attractive blue eyes and a fascinating giggle.

Sean had a problem with the ensuing visit to Rome. He needed a UK passport, and for that, he had to have British citizenship. This he got without much difficulty. For the next meeting, we all brought Union flags, but he didn't turn up that week. After that, he always made doubly sure he wore a green tie.

In Rome, we all kept together most of the time under the fatherly eye of our embryo priest. I went out during siesta time occasionally in order to sketch and got teased about mad dogs and Englishmen. Eileen went gallivanting out for the day on the back of a scooter with an Italian Romeo she had never seen before, to our concern, and Sean and I went to the Russian church every morning. We all went with John the first day, but Peter and Eileen couldn't cope with the strange liturgy and no pews. We loved the music and beautiful icons. Peter and Eileen went to a later mass at the English church where there were pews.

We also teased Sean about getting confused with the currency and magnanimously giving five lire (less than an old penny) for a tip. On the way home, Sean, who had taken the T.T.(abstinence) pledge, had so many bottles of brandy that he dumped some on Eileen to get through customs. We even had our own lyrics, which should be sung to the tune of 'In Dublin's Fair City'.

These four Legionaries,
Those children of Mary's,
Who flew out to Rome once with very high hope.
To see the Coliseum,
And Vatican museum,
And receive benediction from Pius, our Pope.

In Rome, in Roma, in Rome, in Roma,
Singing 'Viva la Papa' in Rome, in Roma.

And one in the morning,
Would rather lie snoring
Than visit the church but a stone's throw away.
The trouble is shaving,
So think what a saving,
T'would be if he joined the good Russians to stay.
In Rome, in Roma, etc. etc.

Beware of the hooter,
When you ride on a scooter,
The lady sits side-saddle fashion behind.
Our Eileen went riding,
With daring confiding,
In Italy's fair youth, so handsome, so kind.

In Rome, in Roma, etc. etc.

The value of lire,
You sometimes might query,
On finance you must keep a very firm grip.
But the waiter's so dashing,
And the ice cream's so smashing,
Me thinks that five lire's not much of a tip.

In Rome, in Roma, etc. etc.

If you come back with brandy,
Be sure that it's handy,
The customs official will soon spot the lie.
So you must declare it,
Though Sean, he might share it,
With the sweet, pretty lassie that's standing close by.

In Rome, in Roma, etc. etc.

Peter and his sister Barbara came back with me to the vicarage at Himbleton. On a glorious Saturday afternoon in late spring, it was idyllic there, with all the wild flowers in the orchard and the Malvern Hills beyond. An afternoon always to be remembered.

A few weeks later, Peter said that he had a fortnight's holiday to coincide with the first part of the school holidays, and he suggested that we went out on day trips together from Nuneaton. I jumped at the idea, although I had no notion where I would get the money from so soon after the Rome trip. I wasted no time in telling my parents that I wouldn't be home for two weeks after we broke up and started saving every penny.

Shortly before our holiday was due to start, I took maps to Peter's house on a Sunday evening, saying, 'Don't you think it's about time we made a few plans as to where we are going on these days' out?'

'Oh,' Peter replied, 'didn't I tell you? Mother and I decided it would do us both more good if we got right away for the fortnight. You're not upset are you?'

'Oh no!' I said. I was devastated.

I spent the rest of the evening chatting with Peter's maternal grandmother, who was living there at the time. She was a lovely old lady who told me about the fish shop and was proud of having served fish and chips in newspaper for many a year. After a polite farewell, I made my way back to Mrs Brown's. I swallowed my tears but resolved that Peter would never know how upset I was. I decided that I would still go up to Peter's house occasionally. Perhaps every three weeks at first and then gradually slope off altogether.

Mrs Brown asked me why I was so red-eyed. I passed no comment and went straight to bed.

The next morning, she said I had to leave as she did not want someone living there who gets so upset and miserable. I went to the YMCA in Coventry for one week.

No. 6 MRS SOUTHERLY

I did not want to go straight home. My parents would have asked me why I arrived back before I had intended, and I wasn't ready to tell them yet. Fortunately, I found new digs without any trouble.

Mrs Southerly was a bookie's widow. She had considerable middle-aged spread but did her best to look younger with make-up and her hair dyed a copper colour. She lived in a Victorian terraced house, like Mrs Brown's, but with a miniscule front garden in an avenue lined with mature trees. Her dining room exuded wealth. The walls were covered with imitation oak panelling, finished by a high picture-rail shelf filled with silver trinkets. The plain 1950s door was beautifully grained to look like solid oak. The sideboard was loaded with elaborate silver candlesticks and bowls. My first thought was that all these must take an awful lot of cleaning! Upstairs was very different. My room had rather tatty bedcovers and no means of heating, which didn't matter at this time of year, but I wondered what it would be like in the winter.

There wasn't even an electric power plug, although that wasn't all that unusual in the 1950s. The bathroom was quite shabby too, and the bath had been painted crudely with some sort of cream paint.

The kitchen left much to be desired. That didn't matter in term time because I had a cooked meal every day at school, but I decided that during the next fortnight, I would be picnicking in my bedroom.

Altogether Mrs Southerly was quite a character, and once I got used to her rather affected speech, I grew to quite like her.

For the next two weeks, I worked to a strict timetable from nine to four, making a series of infant-school textbooks. In the evenings, I did my legion work and went to first-aid classes. Later, I tried to publish my books but without success. This did not matter. I used them for my own teaching, and making them had been most therapeutic.

I asked Mrs Southerly if I could have a bath. She said yes but added, 'You know there is no hot water upstairs. I'll give you a bucket, and you can help yourself in the kitchen.'

I thanked her and carried a couple of buckets gingerly up the plush stair carpet, but I had a horrible bath. The water was only just warm and the roughly painted surface grated against my skin. I would have to go back to the slipper baths. I used them while I was at Mrs Brown's as she had no bathroom, but I had been looking forward to having a bath in the house now.

The slipper baths were quite near the school where I taught, so I could call in on the way home. The warden was a white-haired lady with light blue eyes. She was so well scrubbed that she looked as if her top layer of skin had been scrubbed away. Always with knitting needles in her hands, she was continuously knitting, usually complicated Fair Isle patterns in several colours.

There were a dozen baths in cubicles ranged on either side of the central passage. The control of the taps was outside of each cubicle, so you had to shout for the warden to turn them on or off. We were all told to wipe clean our bath before leaving. The building was lofty, probably constructed before the First World War. High on the roof was an enormous cylindrical boiler. On one occasion while I was relaxing in the bath, this boiled. The noise was horrendous, magnified by the shape of the building. Never had I got out of a bath and dragged on the minimum of clothes more quickly. Did I wipe around the bath before I left? No! I rushed out and crossed the road. Looking back, I was surprised to see the bathhouse still standing. I wondered if the white-haired lady was still knitting, and stories of the French Revolution went through my head. I hurried back to my digs to take off my damp clothes and get properly dry.

I was preparing schoolwork one evening when there was a knock on the front door. I opened it. A neat little man of about sixty with a wallet of documents under his arm was waiting on the step and asked if Mrs Southerly was in.

I said no.

He told me that he was the churchwarden at Stockingford, a village near Nuneaton which was now engulfed as a suburb. He said that he had an urgent problem with the parish hall deeds and that Mrs Southerly might be able to help.

'You are welcome to come in if you so wish,' I replied, 'but she will be about half an hour.'

He said that he would wait, and I showed him into the sumptuous dining room. I made him a cup of tea, and we chatted amicably until she arrived. I introduced him to her, then he sat down, put on his glasses, and spread his documents over the table. I continued chatting while she made another cup of tea, then I retired to my room.

During the following weeks, the churchwarden of Stockingford came to the house frequently. It vaguely crossed my mind that these church hall deeds must be causing an awful lot of trouble.

Christmas was approaching, and the weather was getting colder. Mrs Southerly called me to come down and sit with her in the dining room. I thought this would be a good opportunity to ask for some sort of heating in my room. But she was all of a flutter.

'You have met the churchwarden from Stockingford, I believe?'

I said that I had, and then she continued, 'Well, he is such a nice gentleman, and we get on so well together that we have decided to get married.'

'Oh,' I exclaimed, not knowing what else to say.

'I am afraid you will have to leave after Christmas.'

I agreed to find other accommodation for January, and thought, *At least that solves the heating problem.*

I went to the parish priest, feeling rather sorry for myself. He gave me the address of a lady in the adjacent street.

Three times now I had had to leave my digs because the landlady was getting married. I was determined that the next time would be reversed. I would leave because I was getting married! Not that I had any idea who my partner would be. I was still secretly in love with Peter, but I wasn't wasting any more time flogging a dead horse!

Nevertheless, I did hedge my bets. I put my name down for a council flat, although I was warned that it would be a long time coming up as I could not claim priority. I never heard anything further.

No. 7 MRS ISAN

Mrs Isan's house was built at roughly the same time as that of Mrs Southerly, terraced but humbler in scale and located in a street which was never lined with trees. The living room was still paved with red flagstones, beautifully polished and in part covered with coconut matting. There was no bathroom. The toilet was down the yard, which was completely overshadowed by a six-story-high clothing factory. The kitchen was spotless.

Mrs Isan herself was so different from the flamboyant Mrs Southerly. Also a widow, she was a dapper little lady with grey hair and a rather grey complexion. A conscientious Roman Catholic, she considered herself very morally upright and took a great pride in her cleanliness, albeit she was a child of her generation. The woman next door went out to work and had to do all her washing on a Saturday. One day Mrs Isan remarked to me, 'That woman over the fence must be a very dirty woman. Every Saturday she has seven pairs of knickers on the washing line!'

She looked at both sides of every penny, hard up and proud of it.

She had two sons; one of whom, she told me, had been one of the last four cases of smallpox in the country. He had had a very high fever but survived all right. However, every scrap of her furniture and all her belongings were burnt, and the house was thoroughly fumigated—an event which she seems to have taken philosophically.

Weary and resigned to whatever accommodation fate handed out to me, I retired to my room, which was sparsely furnished, just with an old-fashioned iron bedstead with a hard horsehair mattress and a wash-hand stand. There was also a one-bar electric fire.

My life seemed very dull, most evenings being spent doing very mundane Legion work. My good friend Shelagh, although worried about her fiancé, Alan, still being in the sanatorium, kept up my morale. I did go to the pictures once or twice with Bernard, a pleasant young man from Dublin, but I didn't feel at ease with him. Later I realised he was gay; this was not a problem. If this is how some men want to be, fine, but Bernard could not give me the relationship I wanted. I had come to terms with the fact that romantic love was a luxury in which I would never be able to indulge. All I asked for now was a good father for my kids. For such a person, I would give my all.

All the Legion of Mary folk and a lot of other parishioners along with Mrs Isan went on a pilgrimage to Walsingham. The shrine left me cold, but I enjoyed chatting to various folk on the coach. On the way home, Sean acted the idiot, prancing up and down the gangway with Eileen's shopping bag as a hat and talking nonsense. Peter remarked that he couldn't believe that he had taken the T.T. (abstinence) pledge, but he kept us all amused. When we got back, Mrs Isan remarked to me, 'You like men's company better than women's, don't you? I don't mean to say you are a flirt, you just like talking to men.'

I thought about it, and yes, it was true and still is. I do prefer to talk about steam engines and construction work rather than fashions and shopping.

I was walking down the church path after Sunday Mass when Sean caught up with me.

'I've finished at Wardle's dairy farm,' he said, 'and I'm working for Croft Granite, making kerbstones for this motorway they are building, the M1. It's shift work, but the pay is twice as good, £18 a week instead of £9, and there's overtime.'

I gave him a mouthful. 'You men are all the same, here's you besotted with farming, and just because there's a bit more money in it, you chuck it in for work in a factory.'

I was beginning to quite like Sean, and it had occurred to me that I wouldn't mind living in a farm worker's tied cottage, but in no way could I cope with Croft Granite factory estate.

It was Whit Sunday of 1956. I was sitting in the living room after church when Sean's face appeared at the window. I went out to the backyard to see what he wanted.

'Are you doing anything tomorrow?' he asked.

'Well, no.'

'Come to Birmingham races then.'

'On the bike?'

'Yes.'

'Oh well, OK.'

He went back down the entry, and I heard his bike start. I went in feeling quite confused.

'What was that all about?' Mrs Isan asked.

'He wants me to go to Birmingham races with him tomorrow, on the back of the bike.'

'You'll need some slacks on that thing,' she said.

'I haven't got any. Oh well, a skirt will have to do.'

I went upstairs, tested my handbag to see if the shoulder strap was long enough to go over the opposite shoulder, looked for some small change, and went to the call box down the road to phone my parents and tell them I wouldn't be home until Tuesday.

We left at about eleven o'clock on Monday. It wasn't long before I put on my reading glasses to keep out the flies. The part of the bike ride I enjoyed most was sneaking down the middle of the road past a lot of frustrated drivers to the head of the queue in a two-mile-long traffic jam on the edge of Birmingham.

I found the races an interesting new experience and realised you had to bet to get any excitement out of it, unless you had an interest in a particular horse.

Sean dropped me back at Mrs Isan's and said, 'We'll go over to Hinckley church for Benediction next Sunday!'

'Fair enough.' I hadn't been up to Peter's for some time now, so it would be nice to do something different on a Sunday evening.

When I got home on the Tuesday, my parents asked me what I had been doing on the bank holiday. I was a little bit naughty. I said, 'I went to Birmingham races on the back of a motorbike with an Irishman.'

I knew this would wind them up because my father detested motorbikes, my mother had never forgiven the Southern Irish for having the audacity to leave the British Empire, and they both thought a racecourse was a gateway to hell because of its association with betting. However, I didn't expect them not to speak to me for the rest of the week. I consoled myself by making a blouse and matching blue skirt.

We soon fell into a Sunday-evening routine of going to Hinckley church. On the first two or three weeks, we went a scenic route there and back by bike, but with the longer summer evenings, we walked part of the way through the countryside around Stoke Golding, which gave us time to talk. Sean expounded about the pigs he still owned in Ireland, which were being looked after by some farmer friends he admired greatly. He told me that he was going to buy land in Ireland to start farming himself. This explained why he was working for Croft Granite for more money.

He was now living on a farm near Sapcote, a village the other side of Hinckley. He talked in glowing colours of the farmer's wife, Mrs Pemberton, whom he said treated him like her own son. She had run the farm single-handed, as well as delivered milk, during the war when her husband had been serving with the troops in Italy. I was fascinated to hear more about Sean's life and ambitions. I said that I would like to meet this wonderful woman, Mrs Pemberton.

He took me over to see her on the following Sunday. We approached this really old thatched farmhouse with thick walls made of rubble. It would have been designated a listed building had it survived many more years.

When we arrived, Mrs Pemberton was feeding the chickens, which came running to her from every corner of the yard. She was a sturdy little woman and looked as if she had some goitre problem as she had a large swelling on her neck. She made us very welcome and took us into the kitchen-cum-living room, asking us to sit down, which we did after removing several cats. Cats were everywhere—on the furniture, the window ledges, and amongst the crockery on the draining board. The room was surprisingly light, considering how low-pitched it was with low small-paned windows. Soon Roland Pemberton came in. He was much younger than his wife, who was getting on in years. We all sat at the table, which was loaded with chicken, home-cured pork, home-grown salads, home-made pickles, and flies! My first impression of Roland was that he was very crude. He hadn't shaved for about a week, and he put his mouth right down to the plate to shovel food quicker.

Sean apologised for him, saying it was all due to the time he spent in the war. Later, I found he had hidden talents of upholstery and cabinet-making.

Needless to say, I was introduced to the pigs.

It was all a bit of a culture shock for me, a nicely brought-up child from London suburbia, but I enjoyed it all the same; I was interested to see where Sean was living.

We went to Woburn Abbey and other places down the A1, always on Sean's beloved 500 cc Norton motorbike. Now and again, we did the ton—100 miles an hour, Sean wearing just a cloth cap and glasses and me with headscarf and reading glasses. Sometimes, we turned off to find a secluded spot for a little lovemaking, but I am ashamed to say I was only plain acting. After all, Sean was not Peter! However, we were seeing a lot more of each other now, and I was enjoying his company.

I had jaundice that summer, during which time Sean wrote me three letters, and I realised how abysmal his education in Ireland had been.

The next Sunday evening, we went to a different church, Sacred Heart, Branston, just outside Leicester. All the ceremony and candles seemed a little exotic to me, but Sean thought it was wonderful.

Again, we went for a walk on the way back. Sean said, 'Would your parents give us some help to get started in farming?'

'No!' I replied abruptly, and thought, *The cheek of it.* After a while I added, 'Anyway, I wouldn't ask them.'

We walked on in silence.

Then I said, 'My father gave up a jolly good job in the bank for half the salary as an Anglican parson, and any savings they had they used to live on while he was in training at St John's, Durham.'

The evenings were drawing in now, and the trees on either side of the lane loomed in on us menacingly, reflecting my mood.

When we got back to the bike, Sean remarked, 'The priests in Ireland seem to have plenty of it!'

We arrived back at Mrs Isan's, and he said, 'See you next Sunday.'

I went in without answering.

The following Sunday, we went to Benediction and an evening walk as usual. Neither of us mentioned the conversation of the previous Sunday.

Shortly after Christmas, Sean said, 'The farm next to Pemberton's is up for sale. It's been on the market for some time now. The Youngs can't sell it, and they want to retire.'

'Oh,' I said, wondering what was coming next.

'I've offered £4,000 for it.'

'And where do you suppose you'll find that sort of money from on £18 a week?'

'Oh, there's plenty of money in the bank.'

I passed no comment, thinking, *What's the harm in a little daydreaming?*

About a month later, he said, 'We've bought that farm!'

'*We've* bought that farm! Where do I come in to it?'

'We've bought that farm,' he repeated.

'Oh.' I listened with half an ear as he went on about the single-row cowshed, loose box, grinding shed, three pigsties, a Nissen hut, a Dutch barn, and excellent land.

'And how are you paying for it, may I ask?'

'We've got an eighty-year mortgage.'

'*We've* got an eighty-year mortgage, have we?'

I had been thinking quite a bit about farming. Starting from scratch did seem an interesting challenge. I added, 'I might just help you with the solicitor's fees, but I want to see the house first.'

'We get possession in May,' he said.

'So we do, do we?'

When I returned to Mrs Isan's, she said, 'You are very pensive tonight.'

'Yes, I have a lot to think about.'

I found out from the particulars that there was electricity, but no water mains. The well water had to be pumped by hand, and of course, there was no mains drainage.

When I did eventually see the house, it looked most romantic. It was like a little doll's house. The front was whitewashed, with green paintwork. The stairs went straight up from the front door with a room either side both up and down. The kitchen and bedroom were along the back.

Outside, the first things I noticed were the three muck heaps—a large one outside the cow-house, a slightly smaller one outside the pig sties, and a smaller one still outside the toilet, which was a little shed situated at the end of the washing line.

Sean was obviously assuming I would go along with him, but I wasn't quite so sure. I liked him very much. He was transparently honest and so single-minded. But I wasn't in love with him, and I knew that, if we did settle down together, I would be not only marrying the man but marrying the farm as well.

I got two quite inspiring books out of the library by townspeople who had built up a farm business.

Eventually, I paid the solicitor's bill, and I suppose that was my tacit acceptance. The payment put me into an overdraft, bringing down the wrath of the bank manager on my head for not asking his permission. I transferred my account to a joint one with Sean at the Hinckley branch.

I had some minor enquiry concerning the account, so I phoned the bank from the local call box. To my surprise, they reversed the charge and put me through to the manager. He treated me to a lengthy interview, questioning me about my teacher's salary, my financial relationship with Sean, and how prepared I was to go along with him in his farming project. He asked me to go to the branch to finalise the eighty-year mortgage, which needed to be underpinned by my earnings. He finished by saying, 'A two-horse carriage can travel fast if the horses work together, but if they pull apart, the result is disastrous.'

I was quite taken aback by such a thorough grilling by the bank manager in a telephone kiosk!

Having sorted the basic finance out, the next discussion to be had was when to get married. We decided on the half-term holiday.

I had taken Sean to the vicarage once, and my parents accepted him as a rough diamond, and a good excuse for me to have become a Catholic, but when they heard that we were taking possession of a farm in May but not marrying until October, they became very worried.

Father said, 'You will make sure you never, ever stay overnight on the farm or do anything you shouldn't, won't you, Kathleen?'

It never occurred to me to do this, but I am sure we wouldn't have abstained in this day and age!

Come May, they were highly amused when we took possession of our thirty-five acres and bought a spade and a fork. Then the bank seized up on us!

I was saving every penny, literally, for the farm. I was living on £3 a week—£2 went to Mrs Isan and one pound for myself. Then Sean suddenly announced he was buying a new bike. I was furious.

'I'm not saving every penny for you to blow it all on a new motorbike,' I stormed. 'I'm pulling out of here, and you can carry on as best you can.'

He made do with his aging Norton ZE9024, which he had bought in Ireland.

I cashed in my superannuation to buy our first nine youngstock cattle. It was only £123, but it gave us a start. They would grow into mature cattle. The accountant, bank manager, and head teacher all told me how stupid I was, but in the event, it was the best financial move I ever made. When I wanted to retire from teaching some thirty-five years later and it was found to be missing, they asked me for the £123 without charging me the compound interest they should have done through terrible inflation of the Thatcher period. I expect it was some poor secretary's mistake, but that wasn't my business. I ran and posted the cheque immediately.

Sean made hay while ostensibly on sick leave from Croft Granite.

Sean took his annual holiday to harvest our field of barley. He called in a combine harvester, which caused quite a sensation with the neighbours who were still stooking their corn to be threshed later. The combine would seem archaic now. It had no tank, instead a platform on which Sean and a neighbour stood, filling and tying 140-pound bags of grain.

During the school holidays, besides the continuous job of pumping water for the cattle and the house, I spent my time decorating and dying tablecloths and old sheets yellow to make buttercup-coloured curtains. My aunt Nellie Wells had given me three beautiful large damask tablecloths, which were most inappropriate for us in our poverty-struck state. I dyed them buttercup yellow. The pattern in the damask showed out beautifully afterwards, but how I made two pairs of curtains out of three tablecloths I can't remember. For the upstairs rooms, I just dyed old sheets of Mother's, again buttercup yellow. The double bed she gave me was much more practical. The only other furnishing in my bedroom was a corner unit I made out of the frame of the old milk cooler; we had an in-churn cooler which was considered much more hygienic.

Auntie Hazel sent us a settee and armchair as she was getting new ones. These furnished the sitting room, and I went to an auction and furnished the rest of the house for £2 10s. Never have I had butterflies in my tummy as I did when bidding at the auction.

The first few weeks of the next school term went by very quickly. After school on the last Friday in October, I packed up the last few things I had left at Mrs Isan's, paid my last rent, thanked her for everything, and walked to the station with a spring in my step. Yes, after three landladies chucking me out because they were getting married, I had left Mrs Isan's in my own time because I myself was getting married!

I was going home for the last few days to make my wedding dress.

PART TWO

HOBBS HAYES FARM, LEICESTERSHIRE

MY WEDDING

The next day, I caught the train to Birmingham and then on to Droitwich.

I walked the six miles from Droitwich station to the village of Himbleton, where my parents lived on the eve of my wedding.

I had a light supper and then a bath and went to bed, dreaming of our little home.

It was white pebble-dashed in the front with green paintwork and buttercup-yellow curtains in the front.

The kitchen was built as an extension along the back and was just whitewashed bare bricks. A third bedroom was built above.

Then I heard my father stomping along the landing. He shouted out, 'That daughter of ours thinks she owns the place, she's taken my bathwater.' Not for the first time had I got into trouble for taking the bathwater on a Friday night. But I did think a bride had the right to a bath on the eve of her wedding.

I was married by Fr Dewis, who was our guide around Rome.

I wore the white wedding dress which I had made. I had one bridesmaid, Pat Floyd, a teenager who chose her own dress of lemon with a blue sash. Uncle Leonard gave me away.

We had quite an ordinary wedding breakfast with my parents and just the guests who had taken part in the actual ceremony.

No awkward in-law problems for me as Sean was an orphan!

We went for a very short honeymoon at Aunt Joan's, near Croyden, because we could stay there for free and we were saving up for the farm.

OUR
WEDDING
PHOTOGRAPH

Sean with baby
Margaret.

Margaret, Kevin
and Martin at
Hobbs Hayes .

The only thing I remember about the journey down to London was that the car Sean had borrowed had window wipers working directly from the engine so that they varied speed to the speed he was driving at.

The next day, we went up to London. In the seventeen minutes the train took to get from East Croyden to London Bridge, we discussed how many children we would have.

Sean said, 'Fourteen.'

I said, 'No way, that's not a family, that's a crowd. You want a proper Irish family . . . one priest, one nun, one single girl to look after the parents in old age, and the rest having large families of their own. I draw the line at six.'

I have often thought since that the reason I wanted six children was that I had six dolls as a little girl. At that time, there was a great fuss in the media about the Princess Elizabeth and Princess Margaret Rose's walk-in doll's house. What had they got that I had not? I had a walk in doll's house, the air raid shelter, added to which it had bars along the side where I could hang hammocks for my dolls.

> Dolls were the centre of my play,
> Companionship by night and day,
> Tending them no trivial game.
> I mothered and taught and nursed each doll,
> Mine an ever-changing role,
> Theirs invariably the same.
>
> Betty, the big bouncing bully,
> Valerie, my brown-eyed beauty,
> Daphne, her blue-eyed twin.
> Doreen sometimes took my fancy,
> Bosom friend of little Nancy,
> Iris with the impish grin.
>
> (from my poem 'The Only Child')

In the event, I had eight children—five, then twins, then an accident, John; and after that, I was careful.

Since I have been a mother myself, I have realised what I put my poor mother through. When the air-raid warning went, I insisted on collecting my six dolls from all over the house before going to the shelter. This was until Mother thought of the idea to put all my dolls into the shelter before I came home from school.

RUNNING THE FARM IN OUR SPARE TIME

Sean had told me to keep an eye on the middle sty; the sow there was about to farrow. I had finished stripping the bedroom walls, so I went out to have a look. There were three pink piglets. I was delighted. I hung two pieces of wallpaper and then went to have another look. There were five piglets and another was born while I was watching. I had hardly got back to the house when I heard a horrific squeal. I hurried back to the sty. The mother pig had lain on a piglet. I walked slowly back to make a cup of tea. While the kettle was boiling, I heard another squeal, and another. I rushed to the sty. Three dead piglets! Sadly I returned to my papering. Next time I dared to look, she had nine more piglets, and I felt much better. Twelve was a good litter after all. But then squeals and more squeals! I was devastated. By the time Sean got home, there were only three live piglets out of fifteen.

'Don't cry,' he said. 'It's not your fault. The sty is much too small. I must set to and make a proper pig housing.'

He bought a lot of second-hand kerbstone from Croft and began building. I suppose hoping for future trade, the Preston's farm rep helped him while the wall was low. But the kerb weighed two hundredweight a piece, and his helpmate soon gave up.

He asked me to square up the corners. I was puzzled. I had never seen builders walking about with huge set squares! I measured it up as best I could, but when it came to putting on the asbestos-sheeted roof, it was out by about four inches from top to bottom—something which irritated me for the rest of the time we lived there.

We moved the pigs in, and the other two sows had good litters.

Soon afterwards, while I was hanging out the washing, I was surprised to feel next door's boar rubbing himself between my legs. Sean ushered him to the appropriate sow. He did his duty and then trotted back to his home far.

We never had any more trouble fathering litters!

Memories of Hobbs Hayes Farm. Sapcote, Leicestershire.

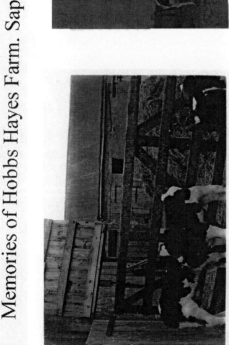

Hobbs Hayes Farm Leics 1958
(Our first Farm)

HOBBS HAYES FARM, LEICESTERSHIRE.

Our Leicestershire farm was lovely to come to. The gently undulating countryside parcelled out into friendly sized fields by mature hedges, veiled by a thin November mist, which softened the harsh tracery of winter trees. The group of traditional farm buildings and the farmhouse with its welcoming yellow curtains looked idyllic. I did not want to return to school after the half-term break.

Now I was living on the farm, we could rear day old chicks under an infrared lamp. Our first batch of 100 we reared very successfully. The second batch was a disaster. We got them at the end of January. The weather was exceptionally cold, and I was overly concerned about keeping them warm enough. I lowered the lamp too much and the litter caught fire. The chicks had a painfully short life. The little shed they were in was also damaged. We had to call out the insurers. There was no problem about payment. However, two weeks later, in class at school, I put a candle too near a winter flower arrangement which included honesty. We had a minor fire, which singed some paintwork. The same insurance rep came out to inspect, and I felt doubly embarrassed.

We bought in point-of-lay pullets. Together with our home-reared birds, we gradually built up our laying flock to 400 hens housed in a large corrugated-iron hut. Collecting the eggs had added to my daily chores. These were not unpleasant jobs, but helping to gather up the old hens and putting them in crates ready for slaughter was another matter.

If Sean or I did it on our own, it was not too bad, but if an impatient lorry driver tried to help, it was bedlam. Feathers were flying everywhere, the squawking was deafening. On one such occasion, I lost my wedding ring. Sean promised to buy me another one but never got around to it. My maiden Aunt Joan was distraught when I eventually had eight children and still no wedding ring!

The need for a proper bathroom and toilet facilities became more and more urgent, especially as our first child was due at the end of the summer. We would convert the dairy next to the kitchen into a bathroom and make a new dairy next to the cow house ready for when we started milking. We electrified the pump for the house and bought the bath, etc., which we put in the small yard outside the back door, awaiting a plumber. The weather was hot, and on many a balmy summer evening, Sean took the opportunity of bathing outside.

As he was still doing shift work, I often had to go to bed on my own. One night, I locked up and went to bed as usual. I was awoken by a tremendous crash and Sean thundering up the stairs. I had forgotten Sean was outside in the nuddy, and he was not amused. He was even less amused when I laughed! I never did manage to convince him that it was quite accidental.

Our bathroom was eventually completed. No fancy work such as tiles, but we felt as if we were in the lap of luxury.

Farming was hard manual work back in the fifties. The sheds all had to be cleaned out by hand and the muck shovelled on to a trailer. The long and lanky Tallis brothers, Roy and Arthur, always helped Sean chuck the muck off the trailer on to the fields. You would hear chatting and laughing punctuated by the odd swear word above the murmuring of the idle tractor.

The tractor would do its share of swearing too, coughing and spluttering when it was asked to move. Dealings were done in hundredweight (cwt) and 140lbs sacks too, weights which nobody would be asked to hump around in the twenty-first century.

The farm was gradually becoming more viable. We had cattle to sell, as well as pigs, although all profit still had to be ploughed back. Sean had sown a new permanent grass lay in our largest field, the nine acres, planning to re-sow the other grass fields in turn. He was one of the most forward-thinking farmers in the district. Our barley crop was doing well. When it was ready for harvesting, he hired a combine harvester— the first to be seen in the area. The farmers around were still binding and stooking their crop, stacking it, and then calling in the threshing machine. Again the Tallis brothers came to help, standing on the harvester's little platform and filling the sacks with grain from the spout.

With the prospect of becoming a family man, Sean bought the most ramshackle van you ever saw. It smelt, had no brakes, and was all but tied together with string. How necessary was the later introduction of the of M.O.T.

He was offered £40 for his Norton bike, but he would not part with it. He let it rust to pieces. I was bitter. Oh how I would have liked £40 with my first baby on the way.

My first child was due at the end of August, so I had the pleasurable job of preparing. I bought vests, yards of Terry Towelling for making nappies, and two Babygros. That was the sum total of my expenditure. I copied the gowns to make several more from various scraps of material, which relieved the boredom of hemming nappies. My mother gave me a beautiful pram, perhaps a little old-fashioned, but large, and it would double up as a cot for several months.

I was ready, but my baby was not. She kept me waiting another two weeks until 3 September. Margaret was a healthy eight pounds and, like every mother's baby, the most beautiful baby in the world! I said that I didn't mind what nickname she acquired as long as it wasn't Maggie. She is always called Maggie. My mother had reared me on a strict four-hourly feed regime. I was breastfeeding but felt terribly guilty if I fed her at less than a three-hourly interval. I am sure this caused Margaret an unnecessary amount of crying.

The cows came up and peered through the window to see what this new animal was which was born into their midst.

My mother was staying at the farm to help, which was wonderful. She shared in the joy of the new baby, but she said, 'Remember, always to put your husband first. Never attend to Margaret until you have seen to all of Sean's requirements.'

I took this advice very much to heart, although I think it was related to my parent's Victorian relationship and my upbringing rather than my own situation. Nevertheless, it echoed all through our family life.

Ever loyal Aunt Joan with her father, Sean and my mother with me and baby Margaret.

THE FARM STARTS TO BECOME VIABLE

Sean had taken a week off from Croft Granite, and I had to persuade or rather bully him back to work, saying that we were not yet financially strong enough.

I returned to my farm chores, and oh, how I enjoyed the wonderful cooked breakfast mother had, waiting for me after I had done my morning routine.

Perhaps I did too much too soon because I got jaundice, so my mother stayed another two weeks. She prepared a wonderful meal for Margaret Mary's christening party and returned home the following morning.

It was hard when Mother had left. There was so much to do, and I had to leave my precious baby on her own so much. It took me an hour to pump the water in the field for the cattle. Then there were the eggs to collect, and as winter came on, there were the cattle to feed. I regretted on insisting Sean to return to Croft. I felt guilty and anxious about my innocent little scrap of humanity. She was my little angel, and I kept her in white for a long time. Somehow, some of her innocence seemed to evaporate when she grew into coloured clothes.

I gave her as much attention as I could when I was in the house. As she got more responsive, I enjoyed playing with her more and more.

The midwife had said, 'Don't worry about not walking out with the baby. Mothers only do that for their own conceit. She will get just as much fresh air if you park the pram outside the window.'

Even so, I would have liked to take my beautiful baby in her lovely new pram just up to see Dolly Pemberton at the neighbouring farm. I never did, not once!

At Christmas, I found a little fir tree and decorated it with lights for my little girl to gaze upon, but Sean always made difficulties about doing anything special for Christmas. It was not until years later that I realised this was due to his harsh upbringing in the convent orphanage. There he was taught that Christmas was Jesus Christ's birthday. High Mass was the only appropriate celebration. Anything else was pagan and sinful.

Sean was so proud of his little daughter that any disappointment he had felt that she hadn't been a boy had long ago been forgotten. Between his various commitments, he loved playing with her. The more she smiled, the better pleased he was.

Besides his job at Croft Granite and his routine work on the farm, he was building two new roomy pig houses with kerbstone, building a silage clamp under the old Dutch barn, draining and gradually laying concrete over the whole yard.

I breastfed for five and a half months. We then decided that I should return to teaching after Easter, and Sean would finish at Croft.

School was a big wrench for me, and I suspected that Margaret would be left on her own longer when in her dad's care than when she was with me. However, I knew that Sean was at least as aware as I was if she wasn't feeling too good, and he thought the world of her. He wouldn't let anything happen to her! Once I got into the classroom, I forgot all about home worries and became completely immersed in my work. I lived a Jekyll-and-Hyde existence.

Sean wasted no time in buying his first cow, Daisy. She was a beauty, but she did kick! She kicked right, left, and centre. Sean had the greatest difficulty milking her by hand, so he overhauled the milking equipment we had bought with the farm. Machine milking did not suit her much better. Sean reluctantly acknowledged that this was why he got her at such a good price. He would dearly have liked to get me to milk her, but I had no intention of going anywhere near her.

Daisy gave us a lot of milk, difficult as it was to get. I had now acquired another chore, churning the butter. This was always an enigma. Sometimes the butter was made in ten minutes, and sometimes it took twice that time; I could never work out why.

THANK GOODNESS FOR THE BANK!

Sean bought a second cow, Buttercup. She was calmer than Daisy. He also bought four in-calf heifers. He had a good laugh at me. I was so ignorant; I thought heifers were male. These, like Daisy and Buttercup, were Friesian. This was the upcoming breed. Most of the farmers around had Ayrshire or dual-purpose breeds. Sean now had to work on preparing the new dairy next to the cowshed for selling the milk.

We had to have our water tested. It was an anxious time waiting for the results of the samples. It would be a very expensive job if water mains had to be brought the three quarter mile down our lane. They could find no fault with our well water. It was a big enough job taking it from the well house to the dairy. Sean also took it to a trough in the field, but I couldn't help thinking if he himself had had to pump water for the cattle for the best part of two years; this would have been done long ago!

One of the heifers was about to calve. It was time for a Milk Marketing Board inspection. We passed. The long awaited calf arrived—a beautiful Hereford X, the same breed as most of our beef cattle. Between them, we got nearly a churn and a half of milk. We were in the milk business! Although only a small start, we felt more secure with the prospect of a regular monthly milk cheque, and it gave the bank confidence. Moreover, the bank gave us an overdraft facility for £10,000.

We were able to buy a more respectable second-hand van and a new Ford Dexter tractor. The tractor was only small, but it was magic. It had a power shift and a hydraulic lift.

We gave our old standard tractor to the youngest Tallis brother, for which the taxman never forgave us. David was at a technical college, studying carpentry. He had done various joinery jobs around our house and gave us his test piece, a stepladder.

I said, 'Thank you, that's great, it must have been difficult to make, there isn't a right angle in it.'

He was deeply offended but accepted the tractor gratefully.

Milking with & Darkie Dog.   Tractor work on Hobbs Hayes.

It was May; the grass was ready for our new venture, making silage. This aroused great interest with all the neighbours. None of them had ever made silage. We cut the grass with our old finger mower geared from the wheels, but our little tractor could show off its lifting skill by buck raking the grass into the silo. Then Sean drove the tractor up and down the clamp to compress it. It looked more terrifying the higher the heap of silage got. Sean assured me it was not as dangerous as it looked, but I was not so sure. Tractors in those days had no cabs or safety bars. The clamp was sheeted down, and the verdict was awaited. What would the cows think when they had their first bite of silage in the winter?

I was just putting Margaret to bed when Sean came in to tell me that the last of our heifers was calving. As soon as my little girl had settled down, I ran through the rain into the yard to see what was happening. She had had twins. Sean was exercising the forelimbs of the second calf to get it to breathe properly. She was watching him anxiously, and she appeared to be neglecting her firstborn. Sean asked me to rub it down with straw. She turned and tossed me on to the window ledge. I screamed and screamed. Sean escorted her into the next shed and shut the door. I still stayed on the window ledge, screaming until Sean came in to ask me if I was all right. I said yes and staggered back to the house for a cup of tea.

We now had a milking herd of six, and the lorry driver was beginning to think it was almost worthwhile coming down the long farm lane to collect the churns.

Winter was approaching. It was time to open the clamp. There was not the slightest doubt that the cows were enjoying their silage, and the milk yield was up. Our silage making had been a great success.

Back in September, I had been very worried that my little girl would be lonely, as lonely as I was when a child. Not only did we live down a long farm lane, but also there was a busy main road at the top. The idea of taking her to a playgroup or suchlike never occurred to either of us even if there was such a thing. She must have a sibling, and soon! But I wasn't pregnant. I bought a book titled *How to Improve the Chances of Pregnancy*. I shouldn't have bothered. Now I was looking forward to Easter and leaving school in preparation for my next child due in June.

For all the times that Margaret had been left on her own, the only major accident she had was with the eggs.

It was beautiful spring weather. I had made a playpen for her in the kitchen yard. I was sitting with her, washing the previous day's eggs. I went to fetch that day's eggs. While I was away, she had a smashing time. I must have left a tray of eggs too near to her playpen. There were broken eggs all over the place—her hair, her clothes, and everything else was just one slimy mess.

A far worse accident happened when she was with me in the kitchen. I had an enamel measuring jug, which was narrow at the base and broad at the top. It was dangerous, and I had made up my mind to chuck it when I got a replacement. That was too late! I had just made custard in it when Margaret pulled it off the table. The hot custard went all over her face. I bundled her under the cold tap, then called the doctor, and cried and cried. Here I was, not fit to be a mother, and I was pregnant again. By the time the doctor came, her face was so swollen you could not see her eyes. She was taken to the local hospital, and I just went on crying. When we visited her the next day, her face was just one big scab. When a few days later, the first scab came off without a scar, the relief was unimaginable. She survived without a single scar.

But she must have suffered shock. Up until then, she had, been saying half a dozen words or so. She never expressed any more until she was verging on three. We knew that she was thinking words, and later sentences, because she would hum the rhythm, but no words actually came out. At the age of three, the words all tumbled out in a great flood of talking, and she never looked back.

It was silage time again. Sean had bought a tractor-mounted finger mower, and I watched it vibrating. I was fascinated by the versatility of the power shaft. Sean had also been gradually building up the milking herd.

We had a cow, Pandora. She was calving, but she was making no effort. Something had to be done quickly or the calf would die. The Tallis brothers came down to help. They brought the calf out, and everyone fell into the muck.

Now it was my turn to be in labour. Kevin was the hardest of all my children to bring into the world. I was getting weary, and with every pain, I was muttering about not giving up like Pandora. The midwife was very surprised to find out Pandora was a cow.

On 18 June 1960, my golden boy was born. Never had I seen such a beautiful baby, pure white hair and a gorgeous golden complexion. He was heavily jaundiced!

The midwife said, 'It will go in a few days.'

I didn't know what she was on about. He looked just perfect to me. Within a week, he was of a good, healthy colour.

Sean was doubly proud of Kevin as one who could carry on the family name.

A WORKING WIFE AND A FANCY ONE

The bank manager's wife gave me a Moses basket. It made a lovely carrycot when we went out in the van, and when in the house, I tied it to the frame of the old butter churn to make a very attractive cradle. My innocent little boy looked so romantic in his basket.

Margaret got worried and upset when she saw him asleep and wanted me to rouse him. I had not realised that she had never seen anyone asleep and thought that there was something terribly wrong with her baby brother.

Whenever she saw me feeding him, she insisted on giving him her two most treasured possessions—a fancy handbag, which I had to loop over his arm, and a red pixie hood, which I placed under his head.

I was happy; as they grew, they would be better and better company for each other.

During that autumn, when Sean was tilling our arable field, a huge hole opened up under the tractor. He backed the tractor successfully but came into the house shaken. Later, we found out that it was an old mineshaft, but the immediate problem was to prevent an accident. Sean got electric fence stakes and wire to fence it off, but we needed something red to warn people of the danger. I searched the house high and low but could find nothing except Margaret's pixie hood. Sean took it; Margaret was distraught. I tried to explain, but I could not get her to understand why Daddy needed it so urgently. It took me some time to console her.

Needless to say, all my jumpers had got badly stretched and baggy during pregnancy, but they were good enough to wear when I was working around the yard. I was wearing a jumper which buttoned down the front one morning when I was untying the cows after milking. Buttercup was in the end stall by the wall. I leant over her neck to release her when she caught her horn up my jumper. She carried me out on her horn. I don't know who was the most scared, me or Buttercup! Fortunately, the buttons gave way as she turned the corner. She dumped me in the muck and scampered into the field. I scrambled up and ran into the house. Kevin was sleeping, and Margaret was playing contentedly. I sat on a stool, too shattered to clean myself up. Sean came in and took one look at me.

'What I need is two wives,' he said. 'One working one, and one fancy one!'

I knew who the working one was, and I had a shrewd idea who the fancy one was too.

The great thing about Sean was that he was transparently honest. Whatever he was thinking came out. I never remotely doubted his loyalty.

I was looking forward to Christmas, determined to make it a good family affair now Margaret was old enough to appreciate it. She enjoyed decorating the house and putting the tinsel and lights on the tree with me. The Christmas stocking was a great novelty.

Then the flat belt on the milking machine broke! Sean had to drive round to all the neighbours to see if anyone had a spare pair of alligator clips so he could make up another belt. I finally found myself washing the dairy utensils after morning's milking when I should have been serving Christmas dinner. However, what did it matter? The children had a good Christmas.

Again, I had breastfed for five and a half months. I returned to school in the New Year.

We had two student teachers in school, nuns. They decided to centre their child studies on a pair of twins who were in my class. I suggested they brought them to the farm during the dinner hour so they could observe them out of the school environment. We made the arrangements. Sean would fetch us from school in the van.

He said, 'We can't expect two nuns in their habits to sit on the wheels like you and Margaret do. One can sit in the passenger seat, but what about the other?'

I had been given a little nursing chair. I thought that would be ideal, so I put it in the van.

Sean duly came to collect us. We all climbed into the van and set off. I had forgotten that the nursing chair had castors. We went up the hill, and Sister slid to the back—down the hill, and she slid to the front. Uphill back, downhill front, all the way to the farm. By the time we got there, we were all so weak with laughter that we could hardly get out of the van.

The sisters were enthralled with our family life. They were fascinated with my children, and the Wendy house I had made for Margaret under the stairs. They revelled in the relaxed atmosphere and laughter over lunch. All in all, they did very little child study. They did not want to go back to school, and I rather suspect they didn't want to go back to the convent either!

It was Whitsun of 1961 and silage time again. We had built our dairy herd up to sixteen, and Sean had sown fresh lays in all our grass fields. We still had one arable field in which we grew barley for pig feed. What had been once a large kitchen garden by the house was used for kale and fodder beet.

Sean had bought a forage harvester and accompanying trailer. This caused a sensation amongst the local farmers as it was the first to be seen in the district. As soon as Sean drove his new set-up out into the fields, we had an impromptu demonstration. Fourteen farmers walked solemnly behind, in deep deliberation about the merits of silage.

Our lane was badly potholed, especially where it approached the house. Sean had asked the ready-mix driver to drop any part load he wanted to dispose by the house so that we could make two wheel tracks. He brought such a load and dumped it, trapping the cars of some of the folk watching the performance in the field. I called for help, no one responded.

I shouted, 'If you want to drive over a mountain of concrete, that's your hard cheddar. I can walk around it!'

Eventually, Roy Tallis came to help. He spread the concrete, but I had to assist with the screening. Never had I been so utterly exhausted, but we laid two very neat wheel tracks, and I was so grateful. I always remember Roy especially for this kindness.

A couple of bolts had worked loose on the harvester. They had to be put right before Sean went into the next field. He took the spout off and asked me to lean inside and grip the nut with a spanner while he tightened the bolt. I lost my balance and was left dangling with my legs thrashing about out of the top. I was giggling helplessly. Sean rescued me but only after he had had a good laugh.

With the increased herd, we needed more bulk of winter feed, and Sean decided on brewer's grains. He ordered a railway wagon full, which would be delivered in three lorry loads. He had to build a special silo and asked me what dimensions would be needed. I had no bushel/cubic yard conversion table. I had to work out the capacity needed from the cubic inches marked on the half-pint baby's bottle. Sean built with more conventional concrete blocks now he had finished at Croft Granite. He decided to put in a rubberoid damp course in case he should want to convert it into a storehouse in the future.

The first two lorry loads arrived in one day. The silo was full. I must have made a grave mathematical error. I had visions of brewer's grains spilling all over the yard. The lorry driver told me not to worry; it would settle down overnight. I was sceptical and went out anxiously that evening to inspect it. Yes, there was room for another load, but oh no, the weight of the brewer's grains had pushed the wall out over the rubberoid damp course by nearly three inches. I ran in to fetch a piece of chalk, and tell Sean of the problem. I marked the amount of slip, and he buttressed the wall with railway sleepers and anything else he could find.

It stabilised, and the silo took the remaining load comfortably.

Sean was boasting to a farm rep about saving the wall.

I added, 'But I put in the chalk mark!'

Christmas was approaching again. I was heavily pregnant. The baby was due the day after Boxing Day. In spite of this, it really was to be a good Christmas—free of hassle, or was it?

The day started off well enough, with the tree lit up and Christmas stockings. Then, unbelievably, the belt on the milking machine broke again, and we had no alligator clips. Never had it broken on any other occasion. Had some pagan gene got into it? Christmas disintegrated into the usual chaos.

The first time I went to town in the New Year, I bought some alligator clips and carefully placed them in a pot on the mantelpiece so that I could put my hand on them the moment they were needed. They were never used!

The midwife was a homely soul, unlike those who had come previously, who were so super efficient that I felt that I was being attended to by a robot. She was younger, a dark-haired lady with mousy features who loved animals. She even came once with dog hairs on her uniform, which might have been a cause of complaint with some folk but which made me feel more relaxed.

It was snowing on 5 January. Sean sent for her at about five o'clock in the morning. She asked him to meet her at the top of the lane as she didn't want to drive down in the snow. He obliged and carried her bag for her. Martin was born shortly after she arrived. He was announcing his presence, as babies do, when there was an imperious knock at the door. Two policemen stood there. They wanted to know what was going on. A motorist had reported a suspicious looking case being transferred from a car and whisked down a farm lane. Martin himself made it known what had happened, and the policemen left, duty duly completed. Martin was born shortly after the Great Train Robbery, and the behaviour of Sean and the midwife had aroused the suspicion of a member of the public!

Martin was slightly jaundiced. Only now did I realise that was the problem with Kevin at birth.

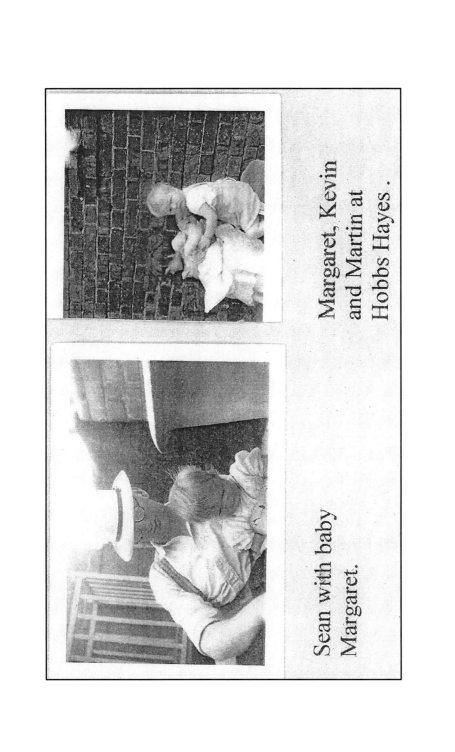

Margaret, Kevin and Martin at Hobbs Hayes.

Sean with baby Margaret.

THINKING OF MOVING ON

On one of her follow-up visits, the nurse came earlier than expected. I had a rubber sheet on the bed and was bottle-feeding. As she came to the door, she must have thought I had a ravenous baby that was making so much noise. It was a piglet! I was covered with confusion. Sean bundled it up in the rubber sheet and took it out. She only laughed.

'A good tale to tell my colleagues,' she said.

Our little doll's house was becoming quite a civilised abode. Sean had painted the outside woodwork a rich maroon, and I had decorated the back bedroom ready for Margaret. We had even installed central heating.

Our thirty-five acres was coming up to full capacity, with sixteen cows and nine store cattle, five sows and our own boar, and always at least one shed full of weaners. Then there were the four hundred chickens, and we also had one arable field for barley. During the sixties, small mixed farms like ours were beginning to become less viable. Larger, more specialised units were going to be the way forward. We should think about moving.

The Ministry of Agriculture had arranged an official demonstration of our silage making, but rumour got round that we were thinking of selling and getting a larger farm, so it was cancelled at the last minute lest the Ministry be blamed for advertising on our behalf. Sean was very disappointed, but a lot of folk turned up anyway. Scanning the *Farmer's Weekly* for suitable farms at a price which we could afford became a weekly routine—and a very interesting one too.

We went to look at two farms high up in the Cheshire Hills. In each, the cow-house and the residence were just one long building, and the fields were more stones than soil. We then visited a Derbyshire farm, in the tail of the Pennines. This was much more attractive. It was a larger farm in a larger landscape. The cloud kissed the hills and embraced the wide-bottomed valley. The farm buildings overlooked the land on the lower slopes. There were grazing rights on the hills. The house was spacious with spectacular views, and the school bus stopped right outside the door. But it was very wet, and Sean was doubtful if the land could be satisfactorily drained.

We reluctantly turned it down. I was particularly disappointed, but it was good to get back to our homely little farm and the Leicestershire countryside, amply furnished with trees and hedges.

I had finished breastfeeding back in June but didn't return to teaching until September. I was glad of the extra break.

This time, I could take Margaret with me. She was officially much too young, but as a concession, she was accepted in the reception class; she was very happy there. We enjoyed each other's company during the dinner hour. The two little boys had to stay with their dad.

I have always been impressed with Sean's care for the children, considering the harsh upbringing he had at the hands of the nuns at the convent. Maybe, if the truth were known, the farm came before his offspring (and his wife). But he always empathised with the children and attended to their needs. They were never given the amount of attention which is expected in the twenty-first century by either of us. Nowadays, the N.S.P.C.C would probably consider them a subject of enquiry for neglect. Children absorb what they need from their environment, and my family doesn't seem to have suffered in the long run from being left on their own so often. I venture to say that it has saved them from being too self-centred.

There were some very heavy falls of snow that winter. Sean couldn't get the van up the lane to meet the bus for school as he usually did. He put a bale of straw on the buck rake and told us to sit on it. Then he lifted us on the hydraulics.

'Hold tight,' he shouted as he drove up the bumpy lane. We did! On three days, the snow was so deep that not even the bus could get through, so Sean took us all the way to school on the buck rake. Margaret accepted that this was the usual way to get to school.

Margaret had been given a big white balloon at her school party. She was thrilled with it, and she was carrying it home with great pride. The main road was clear of snow, but our lane was still shin-deep. Sean was not there to meet us. There was only one thing to do, walk. I had to carry Margaret; she clung on to her precious balloon, but then a sudden gust of wind blew it away. She screamed for me to fetch it as it floated away. In no way could I have got through the snow. She screamed and screamed all the way home. How long is a three-quarter-mile lane when you are carrying a screaming four-year-old through shin-deep snow?

As an adult, Maggie still remembers the cruel mum who wouldn't fetch her balloon.

Christmas of 1962 was good. Margaret and Kevin were old enough to appreciate the festivities, and Martin enjoyed all the excitement, the lights, and the wrapping paper. Our house was warm and cosy, and we had no mechanical failures to spoil the proceedings. Perhaps Sean and I were a little preoccupied. A couple of days before, we had viewed a farm in Lincolnshire. Should we buy it?

We had to decide.

The family at
Hobbs Hayes Farm,
Sapcote,
Leicestershire.

BACK TO SQUARE ONE

On 23 December, we travelled to Lincolnshire to see Stixwould Road dairy farm. The weather was upside down. There was thick cloud at ground level, and the tops of the telegraph poles were floating in a blue sky. We could not see the landscape through the fog. We arrived at the farm. The house looked substantial enough. We took the children down to the dilapidated looking cow-house, and I said to Margaret, 'Now you are Mary and Kevin is Joseph and Martin is the baby Jesus. You must look after him carefully.'

I found some hay and put it in the cattle trough. I laid Martin in it, and explained to the children that a manger was an old-fashioned name for a cattle trough. We arranged that Sean should walk the land while I viewed the house in order to leave the children for as short a time as possible.

As I approached the house, it appeared to be a scaled-up version of our little doll's house at home. The large sash windows looked good, but when I got nearer, I saw that they were in a bad state of repair. The door was opened by a buxom woman with a florid complexion, light blue eyes, and the shadow of a moustache. She wiped her hands on her faded flower-print apron. Confused by me coming to the front door, she bustled me into the living room. I was overwhelmed by the enormous red roses on the wallpaper, which closed in on me. The woodwork was painted bright yellow, and there was plenty of it as there were two large cupboards and a painted picture rail, which wavered up and down, enough to make you feel seasick. The old black range looked well used.

Going into the kitchen, I was confronted by a very large pump dominating a slimy-green sink with no drain and no taps. The pump looked as if it had once served the whole village.

'I thought the brochure said you were on the mains,' I commented.

'Only the dairy, rain water's better for washing.'

'What if it doesn't rain?'

'It's stored under there,' she said, pointing to a concrete slab covering something underground.

She never offered me anything to drink; I wasn't sorry.

There wasn't any electricity; I knew that already, but there was a second range.

Next to the kitchen was a long room with wide bench-high slabs along the outer wall.

'That's where we salt the pigs,' she informed me, 'and we hang them up there.'

I wondered if anyone had been tempted to commit suicide from the hooks in the ceiling.

'D'you want to see the outhouses?'

Strung out from the back door was the dairy, then the wash house complete with a brick, wood-burning copper. Last was the toilet, a dual-seated board covering an underground pit which, presumably, was shovelled from the outside.

She was expecting me to go.

'Can I see the rest of the house?'

Her children were making Christmas trimmings in the sitting room, which seemed quite pleasant. Well, there were more roses on the wall, and the tiled fireplace was cracked and chipped, but these were minor problems.

The hall and stairway would be nice if decorated properly, and the two front bedrooms were large and light, although very tatty. As for the two back bedrooms, they had pokey cottage windows. One had rotting apples all over the floor, and the other had no ceiling; you could see through holes in the wall to the next-door bedroom.

'A bomb did that,' she explained.

I was sceptical. Anyway, this was 1962. I was pleased to get out of the house and hurried back to my children.

As I approached the cow-house, I heard a lot of whispering and shuffling. When I went in, Mary and Joseph were kneeling with hands in prayer, gazing at the baby Jesus.

We played chasing games until Daddy returned, so there wouldn't be much fidgeting in the van.

When Sean returned I said, 'What do you think of it then?'

'It's very run down. It needs a lot doing to it. What did you think of the house?'

'It's very run down. It needs a lot doing to it.'

We all clambered into the van. Kevin and Margaret sat on the wheels, and I nursed Martin. Sean and I never spoke all the way home. We were deep in our own thoughts.

Neither of us mentioned the farm until several days after Christmas.

'What do you think of the eighty-two acres in Lincolnshire then?' I asked.

'Rough.'

'And?'

'There's a field almost as big as this farm, thirty acres, but it's all weeds and reeds except for a patch where he's got kale for cover.'

'Cover?'

'For partridge, he seems to spend most of his time shooting game.'

I learnt later that he didn't only use his gun for shooting game, but he also pointed it at anybody coming up the front path in case they were debt collectors. This could explain a lot of things.

'The ten acres beyond,' Sean continued, 'is even wetter. It's nothing but reeds, and there is a pond in the corner, where they have been prospecting for oil. Opposite the house, there's a field of oats, and at the back, it's just rough grazing. It looks as if it's never been re-sown.'

'So you're not interested then?'

'Did I say that?' he said. 'How about the house?'

I described the house in as much detail as I could remember, but he really didn't believe me. I think he thought I was making it up because I didn't want to move.

'So you don't want to go?'

'I didn't say that!'

'First we must drain it, then it can be brought round, and it is eighty-two acres!'

'You're going for it then?'

'Yes.'

PART THREE

FURZE FARM, LINCOLNSHIRE

STIXWOULD ROAD DAIRY FARM

We put in an offer, and it was accepted. Then the local agent came to compile a brochure. We wondered what we had done; were we both mad! Sean came in for his mid-morning cup of tea one day, particularly depressed. The contrast between our set-up and where we were going was just too much.

'Do you realise,' he said, 'there's no farmyard there. Such buildings as there are, are scattered at random. The cow-house was supposed to accommodate sixteen cows; maybe it did, but half the standings are broken, and the air line and fittings are totally unusable. Two of the pig houses only have half a roof, and the third shed is just a ruin. Why the hen house has been dumped in a different field altogether is anybody's guess.'

'Do you want to pull out then?' I suggested. 'There's still time.'

'Why, don't you want to go?'

'I'm game if you are, but it's got to pay its way.'

'Of course we're going,' he announced.

From then on, we both regarded the move as inevitable.

For the rest of the winter months, life went more or less as normal. I was pregnant again, but I was finishing school at Easter anyway. Settlement date wasn't to be until 3 May, so there was plenty of time.

However, we had to sell Hobbs Hayes. We had any number of people down to view, but the agent had given out the wrong message in the brochure by mentioning the central heating. Because so few houses had central heating installed in the sixties, this gave the impression that the house was much more sophisticated than it was. They didn't even want to dirty their shoes to see the yard. They all went away disillusioned.

Eventually, it was our next-door neighbour Roland Pemberton who would buy the farm. At first, I was disappointed as I was hoping our little farm would still be a separate enterprise, but Sean pointed out that if the acreage wasn't viable for us, it wasn't viable for anybody else either. In the event, Roland made Hobbs Hayes his home farm.

After Easter, we had to start thinking seriously. The first thing I did was buy some wallpaper. I knew there were many more urgent things to be considered, but I could not face living in a jungle of roses.

Sean got down to the more serious business of selling the stock. We were taking the sixteen cows with us, along with Pandora's calf and three other calves which would soon be graduating into the dairy herd. But the pigs had to go as well as the hens.

We did not have to leave Hobbs Hayes until 31 May, but Sean went to have a look at Stixwould Road Dairy Farm as soon as we got possession. He was devastated; the grass looked bad enough in the winter, but compared to our lush green meadow in May, it was appalling.

With no farm buildings worth the name and the house looking even worse now that it was empty, we felt like giving up.

Nevertheless, we soon bounced back. Sean arranged to get the house wired up for electricity, and he got a Ford petrol-paraffin engine to power a generator. Milking was going to be a problem. He bought a four-point milking bale. I asked what that was. 'A portable milking parlour,' he explained.

The move was imminent now. I had packed everything in boxes, with a special, well-labelled box filled with food to keep us going for the first day or two. Sean had got all the machinery lined up ready for loading.

The great day had come. Sean had finished the morning milking; the children were high with excitement. We were going in a convoy—a cattle lorry, a lorry for the machinery, and a covered lorry for the household goods and various farm utensils, followed by the van. I was amazed that all our machinery fitted on to one lorry. We were off to a new life in Lincolnshire.

Unloading went smoothly enough, and the lorries left. Then the trouble began. The cattle took one look at the grass, and then they were off through the hedge, on to the road in search of their luscious Leicestershire pasture. We all had to help retrieve them. Sean barricaded the gap and started to get organised for evening milking. No sooner had he left the field when a neighbouring farmer phoned up complaining that our cattle were trespassing on his land. Sean realised that there wasn't a stock-proof fence on the farm. He penned them in the cow-house, which we were now using as a collecting yard. Evening milking went reasonably well, although the generator wasn't connected up yet, and Sean was using a temperamental little diesel engine.

In all the excitement, the children had forgotten their tummies, but now they realised that they were desperately hungry. Where was that special box with the food in it? We hunted for it frantically. This was no game; it was a matter of survival! We hunted high and low, but nowhere could it be found. Boxes of all sorts—china, kitchen utensils, clothes; you name it, we found it, but no food. Margaret found a round tin, she thought it looked hopeful. In it was a cake made from the Christmas cake mixture, which I was saving for the new baby's christening. We went over to the milking bale (or cow's caravan as Kevin had named it) to fetch some milk and gorged ourselves on Christmas cake and milk.

The next day, the diesel engine played up, and we didn't finish morning's milking until half past two in the afternoon, and we were still living on a diet of Christmas cake and milk. Oh! What a delight when we finally found our box of food.

Sean spent the next few days fencing and trying to make the hedges stock-proof. It was an unending battle with the cows, which were determined to roam the countryside until they found some decent pasture. The cattle always won. We continuously got irate phone calls from neighbours who were getting increasingly fed up at finding our stock on their land.

However, rounding them up gave me an opportunity to see the landscape, which had been veiled in thick fog the day of our first visit. It was wide open, gently undulating countryside with a vast skyscape. The nearby fields were grass. The view from the house was fringed with woodland. The forest which skirted our land at the back was commercial—a chequerboard planting of oaks and pines, the pine being a nurse crop for the oak.

Alongside the farm was Monks' Dyke, which had been much neglected and was meandering like a natural stream. Yes, it was beautiful countryside, but we had to make a living. Just as we were feeling very depressed, news came on the bush telegraph that they were planning a new motorway which would plough right through Hobbs Hayes Farm. This would become the M69.

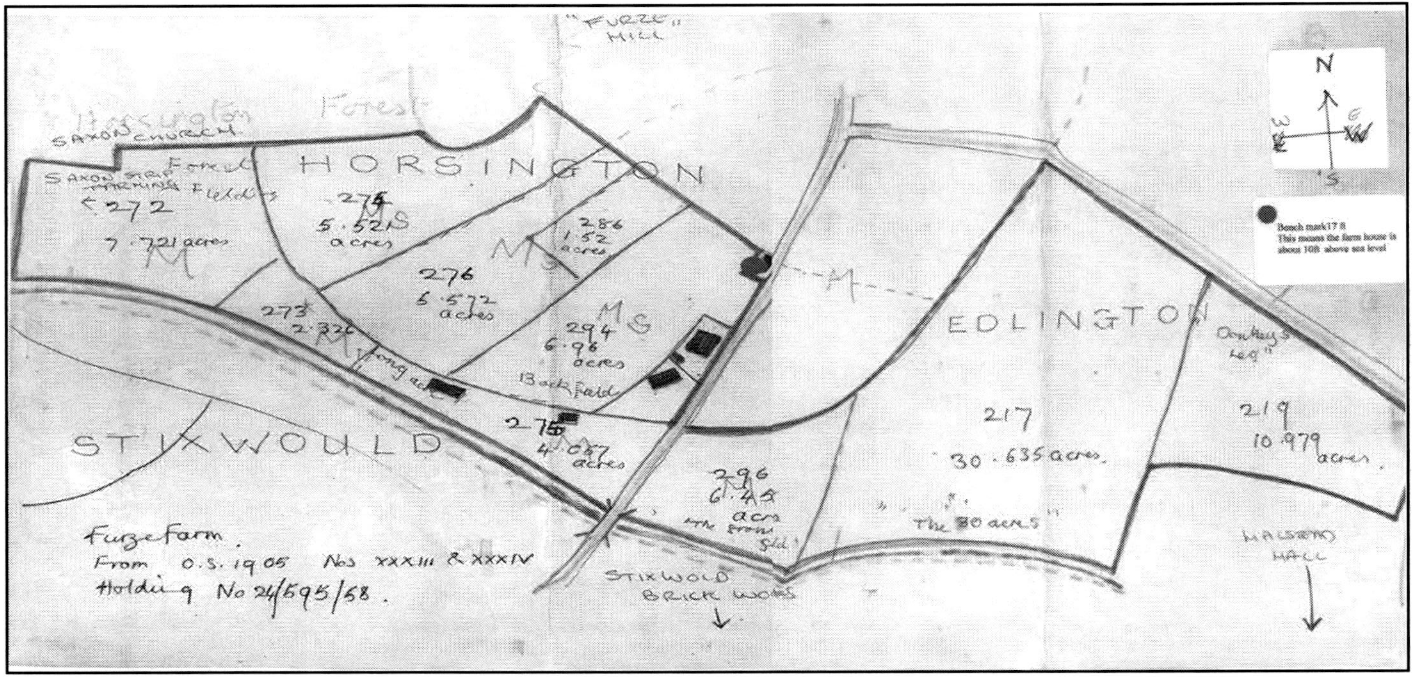

"FURZE" HILL
Forest
SAXON CHURCH
HORSINGTON
SAXON STRIP FARMING FIELDS
272
7.721 acres
5.521 acres
286
1.52 acres
276
5.572 acres
273
2.326
294
6.96 acres
Back field
275
STIXWOULD
296
acres
EDLINGTON
217
30.635 acres
"The 30 acres"
219
10.979 acres
N
S
Bench mark17 8
This means the farm house is about 10ft above sea level
Furze Farm.
From O.S. 1905 Nos XXXIII & XXXIV
Holding No 24/595/58.
STIXWOULD BRICK WORKS
HALSTEAD HALL

What a mercy that we had decided to move to Lincolnshire.

The baby was due at the end of the month. It was to be a home delivery. There was so much to do. History was repeating itself. We had to get a bathroom and toilet installed along with a kitchen sink before the midwife came. We got Mr Jack-of-all-trades from the village to do the plumbing. The workmanship was very rough, but it worked.

When the midwife came on her first visit, all she fussed about was the window.

'I'm not delivering the baby unless you get some lace curtains,' she insisted. 'I don't want to be overlooked.'

We looked outside in vain for those nebulous high-rise flats, but I had to go to Lincoln to buy lace curtains when I had much more urgent things to do such as attacking the roses on the living room walls.

I attacked the roses with a vengeance and a bread knife. I found that the paper was holding the wall together. I mended it with pasted newspaper. I obliterated the yellow paint with white and hung the wallpaper in spite of the ladder being in the way of my tummy.

I was happy. I had bathroom facilities, a kitchen sink, and civilised wallpaper. What more could a woman want? The baby could come any time now.

It was Friday, 6 July; there was no new arrival yet, so I was washing up the dairy utensils as usual. In walked an inspector. We had the regulation of the sink, but I was using a bath at floor level. He asked me why I wasn't using the correct sink. I said, 'In my present condition, I am finding lifting too difficult, and I cannot get the utensils high enough to get them into the sink.'

He was charming; I was not to worry, and he left me to carry on.

Two days later on Sunday, 8 July, Angela arrived.

'In the middle of the night in the sitting room,' as Margaret was only too delighted to tell everyonekeep as is.

My mother had come to help, so by the morning, everything was tidy. Angela was sleeping peacefully in her Moses basket. Margaret came down and gazed at her new baby sister. She made various cooing noises and then said, 'Isn't she lovely, isn't she gorgeous?'

Then she turned to my mother and blurted out, 'Was she a bloody mess when she arrived?'

Mother gasped in horror and disbelief. I had to hurriedly explain that she had seen many calves being born.

On the Tuesday when I heard the postman, I imagined that he had brought me some pretty little cards congratulating me on the new arrival. I got an income tax return and a long winded letter from the Milk Marketing Board. The essence of which was that if I didn't mend my ways and wash up in the proper sink, we would lose our licence. Later in the week, I received a card from the ever faithful Aunt Joan. But that was all. I had had a stack of cards for Margaret and Kevin a handful for Martin, but now just the solitary one. The novelty had worn off!

We could not make silage at this farm. We had no clamps, and the grass was nowhere near succulent enough, anyway. Sean had to get our neighbour to bale our hay. Dennis was timeless; he took every opportunity to sit by his machine and puff away at his pipe, meditating on something or other. Later, we learnt that he was only in his late thirties at the time.

My birthday was 13 July. At four o'clock in the morning, a thunderstorm was threatening. The bales were lying strewn about the fields. Sean was stacking them. He got them into neat piles in the nick of time and ran into the house, drenched, and I whinged because he had forgotten my birthday!

Why, I don't know; we had never celebrated my birthday before or since. How weepy can you get when you have just had a baby!

Sean called me out, 'Go over and have a look at the thirty acres, you'll have a surprise.'

It was radiant with colour, meadow-loving flowers and marsh-loving flowers. Never had I seen such a galaxy of wild flowers of so many varieties.

'That is the last time you'll see them,' Sean informed me.

'Oh?'

'We can't leave thirty acres out of the eighty idle just for the sake of a few pretty flowers. They won't feed the cows.'

I had to agree.

We had the field tile drained. We were surprised to discover that under the heavy clay topsoil was sand. Then Sean began the mammoth job of ploughing. Our little Ford Dexter tractor looked like a toy in such a big field. It could only pull two furrows, and in some places just one. Sean worked night and day until the job was done. The oats were ready for harvesting. Nobody around was willing to combine them for us, so we had to mow them, stook them, and finally get the old threshing machine in. We felt that we had taken a step back in time.

That September, Margaret started at Horsington School. At first, she didn't get on too well socially. Then one of her classmates said, 'Why n'yer spe-ak proper like what we do?'

In less than two weeks, she was speaking the Lincolnshire dialect, and she was welcomed as a mate.

A MEASLY CHRISTMAS

The first Christmas in Lincolnshire was a write-off. Margaret, Kevin, and Martin all had measles. I was worried out of my mind about baby Angela.

The doctor asked me if I had had measles.

'Yes, why?'

'Are you breastfeeding?'

'Well yes, but I am almost dry. I start teaching again in January.'

'Never mind,' the doctor said. 'She will have had sufficient, you have already passed on your own immunity to the baby.'

I breathed a huge sigh of relief.

Kevin and Martin were so ill, they couldn't have cared less if it was Christmas or doomsday. Margaret was beginning to feel a little better by Christmas Day, so I put the tree in their room, with just blue and green lights so that their eyes would not be affected.

Sean and I had no comfort either. We had just had a Rayburn installed. In his hurry to have it ready for the festival, the plumber had made a mistake. The water behind the firebox started boiling furiously as soon as the fire was lit up. It was not safe to use, so we had to put up with the cold until after the bank holiday.

As soon as we got the generator going, we dispensed with the temperamental diesel engine. It was expensive to run, so I only had use of electricity in the house during milking time. We had a temporary wire slung from tree to tree down to the milking bale by the old cow-house.

One day during evening milking, there was an almighty crash. I rushed to see what had happened. Sean had been fetching a bag of cow cake. Breathless we both arrived at the metal bale to discover four dead cows. I rushed back to turn off the generator then made a cup of tea. It was some time before we had the courage to return to investigate. It was only too obvious that the wire carrying the electricity had been oscillating against the roof in the wind.

We thought about insurance, but we could not invent lightning! We just had to be thankful that Sean wasn't under a cow, changing a unit at the time. It made erecting a new building properly wired all the more urgent. We had already chosen the site.

HERE'S TO THE FUTURE, IT'S ONLY JUST BEGUN

W e had planning permission for an umbrella building at the side of the house adjacent to the road, which was convenient for access. It was to be a forty-foot four-bay barn, flanked by two twenty-five-foot lean-tos on the roadside (an extra lean-to on the other side was added at a later date).

Sean had retrieved the necessary hard core from a demolished pumping station by the Witham. We hired two air force men from Coningsby to dig out the foundations for the stanchions, but they made such a meal of the job that I all but dug one by myself while Sean and the children were at church one Sunday morning. We paid the men off.

A lorry arrived with building materials and also the equipment for constructing it—three poles, two pulleys, and an assortment of ladders. The Polish foreman and his two mates raised it with no mechanical assistance whatsoever.

Remembering my botched effort with the pig house at Hobbs Hayes, I asked the foreman, 'How do you square up the corners?'

He replied, 'You take two tapes, and you measure out a triangle three by four.'

'By five,' I added. Probably the Pole had never heard of Pythagoras, and I had spent at least a term, studying his theory at school, yet I didn't know how to square up a building. They hadn't learnt about Pythagoras, but they knew how to square up a corner.

I was teaching top juniors at the time, so I asked them to fetch the bricks from the nursery and said, 'How many of you have garages at home, let us lay the foundations for a garage in the playground.'

A NEW NAME

Now that the cows were going to have a decent roof, we thought we should have one too. I was getting exasperated with having to place half a dozen buckets in strategic places upstairs to catch drips every time it rained.

It was soon completed. With a waterproof roof we were beginning to feel the house was at last becoming a home.

I wasted no time in changing the name of the farm from Stixwould Road Dairy Farm to Furze Farm. The road past the farm was called Moor Lane anyway, and the old name wouldn't fit in the space allowed on the Ministry of Agriculture forms for the name of the holding number.

The land at Furze Farm was almost certainly owned by Tupholme Abbey at some point. It was used as grazing for their sheep, their main source of income in medieval times. So they dug Monks' Dyke (still called that today). Four monks stayed at the then recently built Halstead Hall (our neighbour's house) to supervise the digging of the dyke.

In the front field, I found tile drains—hand-laid and resembling flowerpots (porous pipes tapering at one end), which had been made at Edlington brick works (now Stixwould brick and tile works) from the very end of the eighteenth century. I have often wondered if these were laid before the demise of Tupholme Abbey.

The Monks' Dyke leads to the Duckpool drain, which in turn leads to the river Witham at the last point where water can flow on to the river by gravity, not having to be pumped. Rivers were the source of communication at the time, and the river Witham connected Lincoln and Boston. At Boston, there was a port only second in the amount of business it attracted to London in the eighteenth century.

At the back of the farm just beyond our land was a small rise, crowned by an old deciduous wood—a lovely bluebell wood. This was marked on the 1905 map as Furze Hill. Opposite the farm were three gorse bushes, and furze is the old-fashioned name for gorse.

The Ministry of Agriculture must have had more money than sense as they sent four men in separate cars at separate times from Lincoln to ask if the holding number was to be called in future Furze Farm instead of Stixwould Road Dairy Farm.

We had a farm with a new name, four thriving youngsters, a house which (with the addition of a damp-proof course) was dry, and the skeleton of a modern farm building. The clouds were dispersing; the sun was breaking through and the future looked good.

But there was still an enormous amount of work to do, and I had to carry on teaching. Sean's first task was to build the curtain walls in the barn and, most urgently, make a silage clamp under the central span before the grass went to seed.

We seemed to have an endless procession of ready-mix lorries arriving while he was concreting the floors and yard.

During silage making, he had a break from building, but then the pressure was on again to get one of the lean-tos ready to house the cows for winter.

This involved installing cow standings and chains and an air pipeline for milking. The milk was still being collected in churns, so we kept milking into the unit buckets.

I painted the name of each cow over her standing. Next time they came in for milking, I wished I had a cine-camera. The cows looked exactly as if they were reading their names to make sure they were in the right place. Presumably, it was the smell of paint. Pandora was still our best cow.

Sean next installed individual water bowls for each cow. The tap had a nose pad for the cow to press any time she wished for a drink. It was most interesting to watch the cows inspect this new device. Some experimented and found out how to use it almost straight away. Others watched their neighbours and eventually realised how to get a drink themselves, but Daisy never managed it. Sean always had to press on the tap for her.

We had trouble rearing the newborn calves. At Hobbs Hayes, we had had no hygiene problems, but here the calves were continually scouring. The disease must have been endemic. It was another two years before we finally got rid of it completely.

Another child was on the way, so I had to give my notice at school. At the mid-morning break, one of my colleagues enquired, 'How did you get on at the doctors? Did he say everything was OK?'

'I haven't been to the doctors, I'll leave that chore as long as possible.'

'How do you know when the baby is due then?'

'I use the slide rule that we use for the cows. There is only a four-day difference between the incubation period for a calf and a human.'

'When are you expecting it then?'

'December 29, my grandfather's birthday.'

She laughed so much that we had to delay ringing the bell for the end of play while she composed herself. It just seemed the natural thing to do to me.

On 3 September 1964, Margaret would be six years old. For six years, I had been looking forward to giving her a party with her school friends. I had enjoyed my own birthday parties so much when I was little. We decorated the cake with candles, and Margaret helped make the jellies and blancmanges, which were the high spot of my parties before the war. I went to a lot of trouble to prepare a variety of games.

The little girls duly arrived. They didn't want to play any games until they had eaten. Then it all began!

'Where are the sausages on sticks?'

'Why aren't there any crisps?'

Nobody was a bit interested in the jelly and blancmange. They didn't want to play any of the games I had so carefully prepared.

'Aren't there any balloons? I don't like your party, Maggie.'

'Don't we get any party bags?'

They all went home thoroughly disgruntled, and I was bitterly disappointed. Margaret wasn't too happy either. Maybe I have been grossly unfair, but I didn't give her another party until she was eighteen.

Furze Farm house,-
And its all go on the farm!

MY FAVOURITE TIME OF DAY

Fetching the cows in was the best part of the day for me, whatever the weather was.

There was one occasion when I got caught in a particularly violent thunderstorm when I felt very vulnerable in the middle of the thirty acres, but mostly, rain or shine, I enjoyed the walk especially when I had to cross the fields and didn't have to worry about irate motorists.

I remember one day in late autumn when there was a thick fog, far denser than on our wedding day or when we first visited this farm.

I fell to musing.

> Fetching the cows in the morning fog,
> I was abandoned by the dog.
>> Encased in a lightness,
>>> Of deceptive brightness.
>> Totally numbed by the frost,
>> Meandering aimlessly I was lost.
>>> Bereft of touch, and sightless.
>
> Then I heard a bovine cough,
> The ghost herd led me to the trough.
>> They drank as I waited,
>> My ego deflated.

Grotesque shadows filed past,
I shut the gate behind the last.
    As boss, now reinstated.

This left me thinking, why should I,
Esteem myself superior, why?
    When without education,
    But with perfect orientation.
They knew every grass blade, every weed,
Its place, its taste, its flower, its seed.
    How pitiful my education.

Often we had to take the cows along the road to and from milking. Usually, the motorists were very courteous, but there were the exceptions. The drivers who did try to barge through the herd often got their mirrors bent or broken for their trouble. Perhaps some incidences are better related in verse.

A car came speeding at such a rate,
I waived him down and told him to wait.
The cows were coming out of the gate.

The cows meandered down the lane,
Some in the middle, some by the drain.
He hooted his horn like a man insane.

His hair was on end, he was in such a state,
'I'm best man at a wedding, now I'll be late.'
'Calm down, sir,' I said, 'or worse be your fate.'

He tried to sneak through a space on the right,
The cows nearly pushed him into the dyke.
He tried to squeeze past on the other side,

The cows saw a gate way open wide.
They crossed right over and crowded in,
Wondering what was this odd bit of tin.
Stuck in their midst and jammed on the road,
So one by one, they began to unload.
That posh limousine, once silver, no less,
Was now such a colour, I'll leave you to guess!

Now this story's moral,
    When you're on the road,
    Is never to quarrel
    With the countryman's code.

This driver got his mirror smashed, and threatened us with the police, but Sean said, 'Don't worry, by the time he has had a few drinks at the wedding, no way will he dare to go to the police station.'

After a mercifully uneventful Christmas, it just remained for me to await the birth of my fifth child, whom I was to have in the hospital. She did not come punctually according to the slide rule, but on 12 January 1965. With the first pains, I carried out my now usual routine. I made a batch of steamed puddings to keep the family going while I was indisposed. I arrived in the hospital with not too much time to spare. The midwife slapped me across the face when I made a noise in severe labour then whipped the baby off me before I had a chance to see her. I just caught a glimpse of fair hair as she whisked her down the corridor. As soon as there was no one about, I crept down to the nursery to see my baby. Veronica was the only fair-haired baby there. I was relieved; now I would be sure which child was mine.

I made no complaint about my treatment. I just assumed this was what happened in the hospital. But two weeks later, there was an announcement in the local paper that the midwife had been struck off for being addicted to pethidine, which she had stolen from the hospital.

Margaret had always been known by her full name until we came to Lincolnshire; there everybody called her Maggie. Veronica was too much of a mouthful for any of us, so she was called Roni from birth.

Kevin had started school at Horsington. He kept on pestering me to give him long trousers. He had very smart passed-on shirts and trousers which were originally bought at Harrods. All the little boys where I taught wore short trousers, so I saw no need to get him a new outfit.

I said, 'You can wait until you are at senior school.'

It wasn't until years later when he was an adult that I found out the reason for his being so anxious to have long trousers. His teacher at school slapped him with a ruler at the back of the knees between his three-quarter socks and his trouser leg. He just wanted to reduce the pain!

I was puzzled as to why Kevin's bed sheets were always so filthy, until I eventually discovered that after I had put him to bed, he dressed himself complete with wellies and then settled down for the night. This he did to make sure he would be first up in the morning to help his dad with the milking.

We had been lobbying the electricity board ever since we arrived to provide us with the mains power. Eventually, they agreed on the condition that everybody on the road was prepared to have it installed. We thought this would be no problem. How wrong we were!

Old Mr and Mrs Sharpe had always managed perfectly well with oil lamps, why should they change now?

'Anyway it costs!'

We could see their point, but Dennis, we could not understand at all. His wife was young, and they had a three-year-old child. Both families were adamant. Our neighbours at Halstead Hall had to pay for electricity to be installed at Sharpe's, and we paid for Dennis's.

When it was completed, Dennis's wife called me in to see her new electric cooker. At first I thought this cheek, but maybe it was just a clumsy way of saying thank you.

What a luxury it was to be able to switch on the lights instead of having to light the tilley lamps and carry them from room to room to say nothing of the other bonuses of being on the mains. We even bought a black-and-white telly!

TIME TO MOVE AGAIN?

Monks' Dyke, the major drain which runs the whole length of the south side of the farm was becoming a great problem. It was silting up. Not only was it affecting the drainage on our farm, but the catchment area was eleven square miles, and we would soon be having a lot of angry farmers on our backs. There was no way we could have afforded to bring a big drag along it every other year, which was the least it needed.

We got the National Farmer's Union and the Ministry of Agriculture to speak for us, but in no way would the river board listen.

Finally, Sean went to our local M.P. surgery. Mr Tapsell wrote to us from the House of Commons, saying that if we hadn't heard from the Third Witham Drainage Board in the next three months, we were to let him know. Within three weeks, they were out surveying.

It is now cleaned regularly, and we have never had any more trouble.

We never voted for Mr Tapsell, after all his kindness, but that's democracy!

The year I was teaching part-time at St Mary's at Boston was the best of my teaching life. I enjoyed being in the reception class, and I was there for mornings only. I had hated not being at home when my children got home from school. Now I could have their tea ready for them. I was getting the best of both worlds, having more time with my children and yet keeping an interest in teaching.

But Sean was getting itchy feet. He wanted to expand, and this time, the bank manager was encouraging him.

There was a farm advertised in North Lincolnshire near North Kelsey, which was nearly twice the size of our farm. Sean and Kevin went to see it one Saturday in June. When they came home, neither of them told me much about it. Sean said that the land was much more fertile than Furze Farm, and Kevin told me that the fields were in a long row with a river at the bottom, and we would have a long walk bringing the cows home for milking. I found out a lot more a fortnight later when Kevin had finished his news book and brought it home from school. There was page after page of graphic description of the farm buildings, the yard and the milking parlour. Nothing was said about the house.

However, Sean wanted to go, and people were living in the house, so it was habitable. Nothing could be worse than our experience at Stixwould Road Dairy Farm. We put in a bid, and it was accepted. I got a reference from Boston to present to a school in Brigg.

It was mid July before I got to see Ings Farm. Sean was right; the soil was beautiful rich black loam.

As for the house, it was small, but in reasonable condition. Sean said it could easily be extended. I wondered which would come first, improvements to the farm buildings or the house. I picked some flowers from the garden for Maggie to take to school.

We travelled to Brigg for my interview. I had a terrible attack of hay fever and was holding a gentleman's handkerchief to my nose continuously. Finally, the head asked me, 'You are certain of coming to North Kelsey to live then?'

'Well,' I replied, 'we haven't signed on the dotted line yet, but . . .'

How, I can't imagine, but I knew in that instant that we would never live at North Kelsey.

We did sign on the dotted line, and put Furze Farm up for sale. Our 2,000-acre neighbour made us an unrealistic offer, but he didn't want the house. He would have let it become a ruin. In those days, it was not an option to sell the house off separately.

We had two other genuine buyers who thought it only a matter of courtesy to ask their bank managers for a bridging loan, but because of the credit squeeze, which the government had brought in, they were refused.

Our loan was getting too expensive, and eventually, we were forced to resell Ings Farm at a loss of £4,000. I had to pay off our debts from my salary, which in 1960s meant an awful lot of teaching hours!

I said to Maggie, 'Did you tell your teacher that the bunch of flowers you gave her cost your mum and dad £4,000?' She hadn't a notion what I was talking about.

Later, our neighbouring farm of Halstead Hall came up for sale, but I would not let Sean put in a bid. He said we would live to regret it. Maybe, but to be fair, he never held it against me.

We hadn't got far into 1966 when I discovered that I was pregnant again. My thoughts went back to 1957 and the train journey from Croyden to London Bridge when we had decided on a family of six children. This was my last pregnancy. The family would soon be complete.

With the number of children we already had plus a herd of cows to milk, we couldn't think of going away on holiday. However, we were only twenty-three miles from the sea. Every summer, I pestered Sean to take us to Ingoldmells for the day between milking. The children piled into the back of the van, and we drove off. If they got too noisy, Sean would slam on the brakes, and everyone would tumble to the front. It was a hair-raising journey, but they enjoyed the sands when they got there. I usually slept on the steps while Sean watched them.

This year, a load of brewer's grains arrived just as we were about to leave. The lorry broke down and penned our van in the shed where it was parked. The driver had to phone his firm in the Midlands for a mechanic. We never got to the sea! The children were very understanding; it was I who was so disappointed.

Our collie dog, Dom, was named after a friend of Sean's, Fr Dominic, an Irish priest. Because I loved the country so much but never had a chance to go rambling, my greatest pleasure during the holidays (and when another birth was imminent) was fetching the cows for milking with Dom. He helped but was not as well trained as he should have been.

His favourite occupation was chasing cars as they left the yard and retrieving their mud flaps. We had quite a museum of different types of mud flaps.

For Sean, the high spot of the week was watching wrestling at four o'clock on ITV on a Saturday afternoon. I teased him, saying it was just a well-rehearsed male ballet. However, his enthusiasm was shared by Conrad Brown from the local garage. One day, Conrad arrived in the yard just after the programme. He and Sean indulged in a bout of wrestling, and Dom, ever loyal to his master, took the seat out of Conrad's trousers. He has been nervous of delivering diesel here ever since.

Three weeks before the baby was due, I had to attend an antenatal clinic at Boston Hospital. I was examined by a student midwife. Afterwards, I overheard her whisper to her superior, 'Either that lady has a baby with two heads, or else she is carrying twins.'

The senior midwife came to examine me and congratulated her on her diagnosis. She sent me to have an X-ray. I was thrilled. Two babies, about the same size, were lying symmetrically, heads downwards at the ready.

I could not contain myself. I returned home, sharing hospital transport with several other patients. I went on and on about the wonderful X-ray, and none of them was the slightest bit interested. They were all wrapped up with their own problems.

When I eventually got home, Sean was milking. Although I was so excited, I decided not to tell the children that there were two babies, in case there were problems with the second twin.

Sean was milking Pandora. I said, 'One and one make four!'

'What?'

'One and one make four, one and one make four!'

He didn't get my meaning. I had to wait until the children were in bed before I could tell him the wonderful news.

A few days later, an official-looking person came to the front door.

'Come in,' I said as I looked at the gold letters on his peaked cap, NSPCC.

'Would you like a tea or coffee?'

'Tea, please.'

While I was making the tea, I was trying to think what he had come for. I came to the conclusion that some passing motorist had seen the children helping with the milking and had reported us for using them to further our business. What would be my defence? Well, assisting with the farm routine would give them a sense of responsibility, etc.

'Sugar?'

'Two spoonfuls, please.'

He ponderously stirred his tea; then he suddenly looked up.

'I've heard that you are unexpectedly going to have twins. Is this right?'

'Yes.'

'Could you do with another cot?'

'Oh yes, please.'

'I've brought it with me. I'll fetch it off the roof rack.'

He must have been smiling to himself all the time, but I was so relieved; the cot would be invaluable.

A NEW CALF AND A NEW BABY

All our cows were black-and-white British Friesian, except for one, Topsy. We had rented six acres of grass about a mile away for the dry cows. Among them was Topsy, who was due to calve. It was a Saturday; Sean asked me to walk down and look at them. I always enjoyed an excuse for a walk.

When I got there, Topsy was standing with a calf dangling from her backside by the hips. She was making no further effort, and I was in a dilemma. If I went back to fetch Sean, it would be too late. We would have a dead calf. So I caught hold of its legs and tried to hold my ground while Topsy tried to walk away. Between us the calf was born.

I walked home pensively. Then, *Oh crikey*, I thought, *That's done it!* I was having my first labour pains.

When I arrived back at the farm, the parish priest was standing at the gate.

'Book me a baptism for two babies three weeks tomorrow,' I said.

He looked bemused and said, 'We shall see. Look after yourself,' and left.

I didn't have to go to the hospital until Monday after I had made my steam puddings. It was 1 October 1966, eleven days after the X-ray. By nearly one o'clock, nothing was happening, so the midwife went to have her lunch. Then the baby began to arrive. I would dearly have loved to have brought it unattended, only I was frightened it would slither off the rubber-sheeted table. I rang my little bell and shouted, 'The baby's nearly born.'

Suddenly, it was all systems go, with nurses rushing round everywhere, putting masks on as they went. The first one made his appearance at 1.01 p.m., followed by the other (breech birth), at 1.11 p.m. The student nurse delivered them both. She was thrilled.

When they were cleaned up and presented to me a little while later, they were wearing wristbands labelled Fleming twin 1 and Fleming twin 2. I was angry and shouted after the nurse.

'They are not one and two, they are Patrick and Paul.'

She explained apologetically that they had to be labelled immediately to avoid confusion. She duly gave them their names after confirming that the older twin was to be Patrick. 'It could be legally important,' she added. *In a fairy story,* I thought!

Another nurse was very concerned because my husband hadn't shown up. I wasn't bothered. I told her he'd come at about eight o'clock when he had finished milking, which he did.

I was so happy my family was complete, not six children but the perfect number, seven. And what a wonderful way to finish a family, no lonely only child waiting to go to school and no lonely only child still at home when the others were out in the world. And it would be quite nice not to have another pregnancy when all food tasted like cardboard!

I was so happy I made up a little ditty.

The new dads came streaming in the ward
Bringing kisses, flowers, and sweet accord.
Unvisited, I'm unperturbed,
My man milks his dairy herd.

I'm grinning like a Cheshire Cat,
Preening myself, believing that
Of all the mums that walked this earth,
I alone gave double birth.

I think if I was asked, What was the best day of my life? I would say 1 October 1966.

THE COMPLETE FAMILY?

Shortly after the twins were born, Sean's friend, Fr Dominic came to stay. He had spent much of his life working on Liverpool docks with Irish Catholic seamen, often intercepting them as they came ashore in order to take their wages to their wives before being blown at the dockside pubs.

Now he was retired and a trifle corpulent. He found my small children rather trying, especially their high-pitched voices. Although I enjoyed his company, I found his stay a strain and was not sorry to see him packing his bags.

A health visitor arrived. She was a neat little woman with ginger hair, sharp features, and a suspicion of freckles. She spoke with a broad Northern Irish accent. She explained that twins were automatically registered as at risk and examined both babies. She found them to her satisfaction and sat down to talk to me about childcare as health visitors do.

Fr Dominic came in to thank me for my hospitality. He turned to her and said, 'Top o' the morning to you.'

She ended the conversation abruptly, picked up her bag, and went. I never saw her again, or any other health visitor for that matter.

When we first came to Furze Farm, the house seemed quite big after the doll's house which we had left at Hobbs Hayes, but with seven children, it was just about adequate. We slept in one front bedroom;

the three girls, in the other. The two older boys shared one back bedroom while the twins had the other. These two rooms were very dark, with just the tiny cottage windows. All the windows in the house needed changing. I had hoped that the beautiful old sash windows at the front could be repaired, but that proved to be much too expensive. Instead we had very basic modern windows installed. Builders we called Bill and Ben did the work. They both enjoyed a bit of horseplay. Ben dangled Roni by the ankles from an upstairs window. She giggled, but I was terrified. Sean told me not to worry, but had I known that shortly afterwards, Ben would commit suicide, being of unsound mind, I would have been even more frightened.

However, we now had a lovely, light house.

ONGOING IMPROVEMENT

The ongoing improvement to the land was the drainage. It took us nine years to cover the whole farm. Our first effort on the thirty acres was not altogether successful. We did get some sort of grass crop, and sadly, our wild flower garden never returned. The contractor only had a trailed drainer which, after all his efforts, made it impossible to get the levels spot on. Neither had Monks' Dyke been deepened. The later tile drains were laid by the big Dutch self-propelled machines, which were more accurate. Also, now the outcomes could be deeper.

When they were working on the field in front of the house, they turned up some ancient tile drains which I have never been able to date. Some were flowerpot-shaped, and others semicircular with flat bottoms. I would think one of these types was laid by the monks who dug out the dyke. What a job to do by hand!

Most of the trenches needed porous filling to help take the water away, but on the far side of the farm, the subsoil was sand, much to our surprise.

In one of the deep cuttings near the dyke, the children found some really gooey blue clay. They made pots and ashtrays out of it, and asked if they could fire them. I damped down the coke on the Rayburn and put them in the firebox. To my utter amazement, and that of the children, they came out as red brick. I never knew that red bricks were made from blue clay.

This solved a mystery for me. I had often wondered why a patch of ground with a deep pond in it, about half a mile up the road, was called brickyard. I now realise that this was where they probably made the bricks for the fifteenth-century brick mansion Halstead Hall.

When Sean had sown the fields with new grass lay after they had been drained, the improvement was quite spectacular. However, we had lost a bit of history. In the forest at the back of the farm is the site of a Saxon church. On our field next to the forest was what appeared to be the contours of Saxon strip farming. Now they are all ploughed out.

We do still have another historic feature. The route of a minor Roman road is marked by the row of oak trees alongside the thirty acres. Maybe it is the ancient hard-core base that has made them grow offset.

Baling and fetching in the straw during the school summer holidays was the big event of the year. I suppose it was the nearest thing the children had to a holiday. Although it was hard work, it was made much more enjoyable for them because we were often joined by the Mitchell family. They had three boys—Robert, David, and Micheal, similar in age to our children. Kevin and Martin in particular became Robert's lifelong friends.

We grew little or no corn ourselves. So we had to fetch the straw from farms, sometimes quite a distance away. This made an outing in itself, and we usually took a picnic with lemonade and always orange juice and glucose to restore flagging energy.

The baler left the bales strewn all over the field. We had to stack them in eights or tens, ready for Sean to fork them on to the trailer, where they were placed very precisely in order to bring the load safely back to the farm. Kevin considered himself the expert stacker.

When we reached home, the trailer had to be unloaded, and the straw stacked in the barn. Again, Sean was the only one strong enough to lift the bales with a fork, so we had to do the rest of the work.

I have always been frightened of heights. The higher the stack in the barn got, the more scared I got at the prospect of coming down. It was even worse when the ladder wouldn't go to the top of the stack, and I had to climb down the first two layers of bales before I could reach the top rung. It was dangerous, just as dangerous for Kevin and Maggie as for me, but because they were not frightened, they were more sure-footed. When I finally got on the ladder, Sean would wobble it, I would scream, and the children would laugh. I had to threaten never to help with the bales again to make my mischievous husband behave himself.

The Mitchell children's father was very tall. And blind. He was standing on the bales one day, and the wire which carried electricity to the house was just about neck height. We all shouted, '*Duck*.' He didn't know what he had to duck for, but he did and saved his life!

It bothered me that I did so much more for my infant class at school than for my own children. I decided I must make more time for them. In the summer holidays of 1968, we got together a little play about Hansel and Gretel, which we planned to stage in the hall on a bank holiday on Monday with the Mitchell family as our audience. The great day arrived, but there were an unprecedented number of bales which needed bringing home. We never had time to show our play. The children weren't a bit bothered; only I was disappointed. As adults, the girls have remarked how much they enjoyed doing the play regardless of the failure to show it. As a teacher, this has made me wonder how many school plays are put on for the teacher's conceit rather than the children's benefit.

THE UNWANTED CHILD

Paddy and Paul were not identical twins, far from it. Their individuality became more apparent as the months went by. Paul was walking at least three months before Paddy, and he was far more adventurous than his twin when it came to clambering about.

They started talking quite early but in a language of their own. They chatted away to each other nineteen to the dozen, but I had no idea what they were saying. Roni, they called Wog-wog, and Angela was Yan-yan. Wog-wog and Yan-yan had to translate for me. It took a few months for them to learn their second language, English.

'Sean,' I said, one morning early in 1969, 'I've missed my period, and you know what that might mean?'

'Is that something so terrible?'

'Well, I suppose not, but . . .'

'I told you they say in Ireland, a family never finishes with twins!'

From then on, we began to look forward to our eighth child and considered the practicalities.

I still had one cot, which I had opened out to make a playpen, but the beautiful old-fashioned pram which my mother had given me was in pieces. The chassis was serving as a go-cart, and the body was now a boat to sail on the Boston Deeps, a short stretch of Monks' Dyke near where the cattle drank, which was deeper than the rest.

Nevertheless, I thought, *there's plenty of time yet, and I shall enjoy making sheets and blankets, and baby grows from bits and pieces.* However, I made a firm resolution not to be so careless in future!

We lived too far from the village for our children to play with their friends out of school, so they had to make the best of each other's company. A favourite place for playing was underneath the beautiful old chestnut tree in the field behind the house, where we had put a swing.

During milking in the middle of a storm, Sean became exasperated because the lightning kept on knocking off the trip switch. The suction went, and the milking clusters fell off, frightening the cows.

Sean asked Martin to stand by the trip switch and switch it on immediately when it went off. I gave him a big bar of chocolate all to himself. He was delighted at the prospect of not having to share it with his brothers and sisters. This made him quite willing to do the job.

Later we found that the lightning had struck our chestnut tree. We were all sad to see our lovely tree dying, but I was appalled when I realised what danger I had put Martin in.

Was there ever such an irresponsible mum!

Sean had asked us all to trample on the edges of the silage clamp where he could not roll it with the tractor in order to force out all the air. The children thought this fun at first but soon got bored, and it was left to me to finish the job on my own. I put Paddy and Paul behind the long barrier which crossed the yard where I could see them from the clamp, and they would be safe from the cows crossing the yard after milking.

The twins were having great fun, playing chasing games when suddenly there was panic. At the far end behind the barrier was a muck heap which, in the heat, had formed a hard crust. Paul was chasing Paddy up the heap, and both twins were sinking in. I screamed for Sean, but he could not hear me because of the noise of the milking machine, so I rushed down, still screaming. I knew that, if the crust wouldn't stand their weight, it certainly wouldn't support me. With adrenaline strength, I hauled across one of the planks used for laying concrete and plonked it on the muck heap to spread my weight. I dragged first Paul and then Paddy.

I hadn't stopped screaming when Sean finished milking and switched off the motor. He at last heard me and came into the yard. He roared with laughter at two little boys covered in muck and surrounded by hundreds of tiny flies. I was utterly exhausted, too weak at the knees even to walk. Sean had to take them to the tap to hose them down.

I didn't trample down any more silage that day!

Sean bought a brand-new barrow, which happened to arrive on the twin's birthday. Paul was in the yard when it was delivered. He assumed it was a birthday present for him. He started shovelling in any rubbish he could find. He kept this up for several days. Patrick never volunteered to help. Instead he stood with his hands on his hips, saying, 'Hard work is easy when you're watching.' A phrase which has been echoed by the family ever since!

It was getting near the time for the new baby's birth. I had lied about the expected date of arrival, saying that it was ten days later than it was in order to get the maximum maternity leave and time off from school. I kept this deception up with everybody—friends and medical staff alike, except for the dentist.

I was sitting on his chair when he said, 'And when is the baby due?'

'Today,' I blurted out. He bustled around and got me off his premises as quickly as he could.

John was born on 26 October 1969, precisely ten days late. Just as I had decided that I should confess to the nurse, she said, 'You are clever, producing the baby dead on time. Not many mums achieve that!'

He was born at Wyberton, Boston, while the new Pilgrim Hospital was being built. It was the worst year that a baby could have been born because the midwives expected them to be born Monday to Friday. The woman next door to me in the ward was given a pill to bring her baby before the weekend started. But the baby wasn't lying straight in her womb, and nature didn't have time to turn it around. She had about thirty-six hours of severe labour pains instead of the expected six or seven.

Also the sister wanted me to say if I was breastfeeding or bottle-feeding, but I hadn't enough milk after eight children to breastfeed, so I wanted a supplementary bottle. This she wouldn't give me. When the gynaecologist visited the ward, he asked me if I had any complaints. I said, 'Yes, three. You can hear women screaming in the labour ward from the ordinary ward, where the women who have high-blood pressure and are nervous about having their first babies are. I am not happy at the process of delivering babies Monday to Friday as I thought babies came when they were ready and not to order, and finally I wanted to breastfeed as much as possible but did not get a supplementary bottle when I asked.'

Doctors have a lot to say, and after he had gone, the sister came to me every feed to ask how many ounces of bottle feed I required. This was a definite improvement.

It was Sunday, and the Salvation Army serenaded John's arrival, playing underneath the hospital window.

Martin, Angela, and Roni had each been farmed out to different friends to relieve the pressure on Sean. I wrote to each of them individually on all eight days I was in hospital. I also made several pairs of knickers for the girls, but when I got home, I found they were all too small; occupational therapy I suppose.

The family is growing-
in more senses than one!

On Christmas Eve, I had eight stockings, no, seven stockings and one baby's sock all lined up in my bid for Father Christmas to fill. First, I put a table tennis ball in the little sock, then an orange, apple, and banana in each of the stockings, followed by individual packets of cereal for tomorrow's breakfast. I fetched the other items—pencils, crayons, etc. Then I sat on the end of the bed and thought, *What am I doing? These children are growing up. Margaret will be going to the grammar school this coming year, and Kevin the year after, yet we are still playing at Father Christmas. The farm won't always be the centre of the universe, neither should it be. It will just be the pinpoint of where their individual lives began.*

Sadly, I finished filling the stockings and hung them on the appropriate beds and put the tiny sock with its ping-pong ball on the corner of the cot. Next year, there would not be eight stockings for eight children. For me, it felt like the end of an era, even if for John it was just the beginning.

By the way, John is a smashing table tennis player!

THE EXTRA MILE

After the philosophy of Christmas Eve and the excitement of Christmas Day, I came down to the mundane routine with a bump on Boxing Day. I had two day's nappies to wash. I had thought my troubles had ended now that I had a twin-tub washing machine, but I found it bothersome and had reverted to hand washing.

My housework was minimal, and I am sorry to say you could often know what season it was by looking at the kitchen floor. I had other priorities.

Our diet was chronically unimaginative—whatever was quickest to prepare, although always home-cooked. Every day, I made a resolution to make a varied evening meal, but I finished up putting a rice pudding or a bread-and-butter pudding in the Rayburn oven to cook while I did my outside chores. After which, I helped the children with their piano practice.

Sean was much more musical than I was, but he couldn't play an instrument. I knew the basic theory and could teach them initially before passing them on to a qualified piano teacher. I also enjoyed helping them with their reading and various school projects.

When we first came to Furze Farm, there were several overgrown hedges at the back of the house. An agricultural advisor came to help us plan our business. He was so taken with the little secluded plots that he said our best option was to create an upmarket caravan site.

This idea appealed to neither of us. For practical farming, most of the hedges had to be grubbed up. This was done without delay, making the fields a workable size. Of the remaining hedges, there was a particularly attractive one, which ran down from the old cow-house to the forest on the perimeter. It had a pond part way along and three beautiful oak trees. Sean wanted to pull this one up too, but I could not see any necessity to do this. We agreed to leave it, at least for a while.

The school holidays had begun, and the weather was very hot. A cow had gone missing, and Sean asked Angela and me to look for it. We searched all around the farm, peering in through the hedges again and again. We combed the forest and looked in our neighbour's fields. We carried on searching for three days, but we couldn't find her.

The only part of the farm which still hadn't been under drained was the field by the forest and the land adjacent to the dyke. The ground was soggy, and the sooner the work was done, the better.

Sean announced, 'That long hedge must go. It will interfere with the drains.'

The drainage contractor came and insisted that the hedge had to be removed before he could start work. I was still sceptical. The heavy machinery came in, and I saw my beautiful hedge ruthlessly grubbed up.

When the digger driver came to the pond, he called out, 'Hey, have you lost a cow?'

The wretched beast must have had a horrific death. The weather being so hot, the pond was partially dried up, and she had sunk right into the middle in an effort to quench her thirst. Angela and I had been looking for a black-and-white cow, but of course, she was mud coloured. Sean said, 'I told you that hedge should have been pulled out years ago.' Maybe, but I still miss that hedge when I go for my morning walk.

After selling some cattle at market one day, Sean came home with a big surprise for the children. He had bought a pony. Silver Star was silver-grey dappled, supposedly broken in, but we soon found that he had a mind of his own. Margaret, Kevin, Martin, and Angela all took turns riding him, but when he decided it was time to lie down, he did, whether anyone was on his back or not! They all shouted for me to have a go. I got up on his left side and fell off on his right. Everyone laughed, but I never tried again. I had had enough traumatic experiences with animals at Hobbs Hayes. Martin was the first to master him, but eventually, they all did. They used to ride him over to see the Mitchell family who lived about two and a half miles away.

At Horsington School fancy dress competition, they went as 'Uncle Tom Cobley and all' going to Widecombe fair. Mercifully, he only had to carry Angela, Roni, and the twins, with Martin leading him.

They won. 'Well done, Silver Star.'

The children always shone at the fancy dress show—the following year as 'Robin Hood and his merry men' and then as 'Dad's army'.

There was another family with whom we frequently exchanged visits. Olive and Roy came from Sleaford on their motorbike; the three lads packed into the sidecar. Sometimes, they stayed in the caravan in our garden.

On such occasion, a lad from down the road, known simply as the Village Horror came to play. I thought to myself, *Give the lad a chance, a child should never be labelled.*

He hadn't been here more than a few minutes when I heard the kids all shouting.

'Don't do that, our dad will murder you!'

He was mixing the sand and gravel which Sean had told them must be kept separate. I told him off in a civilised way and placated Sean. Presently, Roni came in saying, 'I don't like the smell in the caravan.'

I rushed out. The Horror had turned on all the Calor gas appliance, unlit of course. I turfed all the children out of the caravan and chased the lad at least a hundred yards up the road screaming, 'Clear off and don't you ever, ever show your face anywhere near here again.'

So much for my principles!

A NEW MILKING PARLOUR,
A NEW TRUMPET, AND NHS SPECS

Christmas had come round again. Sean had a very severe attack of flu. The house was so cold; I brought a bed down to the sitting room and lit a huge fire and kept him supplied with hot water bottles. Kevin and I struggled through the milking on our own. I could not have managed without Kevin's help. I came in exhausted and thought, *Christmas this year is a write-off, so we'll just have a fry-up for lunch.*

Then everything changed. The Mitchell family arrived—Dad with a bottle of sherry, Mum with mince pies and sweets for the children. We had a fantastic three hours, the blazing fire adding to the festive spirit. Even Sean brightened up in the company. After they left, I made a mixed grill, which the kids enjoyed so much more than the traditional fare. Then we opened our presents as usual. All in all, it turned out to be one of the best Christmas times we ever had.

Our milking set-up was beginning to look decidedly old-fashioned. Most self-respecting farmers were now milking in parlours. Our cows still had standings. We milked into churns, but it was becoming apparent that the churn lorry's days were numbered and all milk would be collected in bulk. We would have to modernise.

We decided to install a six abreast parlour in the extra lean-to, use the existing cow-house as a collecting yard, and build an adjoining shed to house a bulk tank. Sean did practically all the work himself. The last job was rendering the walls for hygiene purposes. Most of Sean's workmanship on the farm was good even though when it came to doing jobs in the house, 'what was good enough for the cows was good enough for the wife!'

Plastering was a different matter. His effort was appalling, yet he thought it quite adequate. I knew it would never pass inspection, so I sneaked out while he was eating his dinner and plastered about six square yards, not well enough for a dwelling but a considerable improvement on Sean's work. Sean went out and finished the job. Nothing was ever said, but he wasn't going to be shown up by a mere woman!

The inspector duly came. The plastering passed without comment. Next, Sean had to run water through the milk pipeline into the tank to demonstrate that everything was working efficiently. There were no problems. The tank had to be calibrated. To do this, the inspector had to get under the tank to level the legs. Sean had forgotten that there was still water in the tank from the pipeline and inadvertently pulled the plug, bestowing upon the smartly dressed official an un-ceremonial baptism. He was not amused; I was. He happened to be the same chap who sent that very unwelcome letter just after Angela was born!

Milking in the parlour might have been more efficient, but we lost that personal relationship with the cows. All we saw of them now were their backsides!

However, I took the opportunity of no longer assisting with the milking. There were no longer the four-gallon stainless-steel buckets to carry and lift into churns. The children took over from me, taking turns to help their dad with the milking. But they missed the lorry driver who collected the churns, playing football with them every day while I made him a cup of tea.

When Martin was helping Dad carry the milk rubbers over to the dairy to be washed, he would blow through them. He found the open notes so that he was able to play a tune. I thought that any child who could play a tune on a milking tube deserved a proper instrument. I spent £40 on a trumpet. To me, this was a fortune, and I thought it would be money down the drain as he would probably abandon it after the novelty had worn off. In the event, it was the best £40 I have spent as playing the trumpet has proved to be Martin's lifetime hobby. He had failed at the eleven-plus exam, and while Maggie and Kevin had gone to grammar school, Martin had to go to the secondary modern school. He became very demoralised by this, but his skill at trumpet playing boosted his self-esteem again. He even went on to play in the town band!

The next major improvement to the house was the installation of central heating serviced by a straw-burning boiler. This was Sean's pride and joy as this type of boiler was still very much at the pioneering stage. There were no others for miles around and very few in the country at the time. He showed it to all the farm reps and any other visitor who happened to come by. The boiler was a hungry beast, consuming up to eight standard small straw bales a day. It may have saved us money, but it made a lot of extra work. It is probably because straw boilers are so labour-intensive to run that they never took off!

Roni was a lovely little girl, quite chubby, with straight blonde hair and blue eyes. She was always smiling, well nearly always. At school, she was a favourite with the dinner lady, who nicknamed her Pudding because she always enjoyed her second helpings. But she didn't get on very well with her teacher. She had a sight problem and had to wear National Health glasses, which she hated. She was continuously breaking them. I said very magnanimously, 'If you can keep your glasses for a whole term without breaking them, I will consider buying you a pair privately, and you will be able to choose the frames.'

They were broken within a fortnight. It wasn't until she was an adult that I found out that she thought her teacher was picking on her because she was wearing NHS glasses, so every time she was told off, at the next opportunity, she would deliberately stamp on them. She had to cope with another hazard too. We had reared half a dozen cockerels. The bully among them had made himself leader, and he became quite vicious. He took a particular dislike to Roni. When she left for school in the morning, he would try to chase her up the road and nip her at the back of the knees between her long socks and her skirt.

When we said we were going to kill him for Christmas dinner she wasn't a bit sorry. It was just another reason for looking forward to Christmas.

Roni had a favourite calf called Jimmy. She took him on the front lawn to graze. Whether it was because of this preferential treatment or not, I don't know, but Jimmy became a very special calf.

This is his story:

Jimmy was our favourite calf,
As every day we had to laugh,
At Roni with him on the halter,
Her little hands would never falter
As she guided him (when he didn't lead her),
Who was boss, we were never quite sure.

As he came to castrate him, the vet said, 'He's good,
If we left him to breed, I'm sure that he would
Have innumerable calves to his credit
That would grow into stock of considerable merit'
Thus in time he matured as a noble sire.
What more could the cows and heifers desire?

He grew majestic, with massive white head
And bulking shoulders, a man might dread.
James Furze the First we named him.
(Though the pedigree folk disclaimed him)
He was as soft as a kitten for all his great size.
He liked best a scratching between the eyes.

We're sad, so sad, now he has to go.
He tramped up the horsebox, and although,
It's still early days in November,
And he has a reprieve until December,
When he will appear in a local fat show,
We're all very sad now he has to go.

Angela was of slighter build than Roni. She had grey-blue eyes and lovely wavy brown hair.

The problem was that, when I was so rushed in the morning and wanted to comb her hair ready for school, she created such a scene that we cut it very short, something for which she has never forgiven me. (She is a mother herself now and has a little girl she calls her Princess. Maya has beautiful long golden hair, which her mum lovingly brushes, however pushed for time she is. I suppose we all learn something from our mums even if it is only by negative example.)

Angela was a very honest little girl.

A police car pulled up at the gate.
We all rushed out, we couldn't wait.
'What's wrong?' we shouted. 'What's our fate?'
The collie chased his tail.

Mother had the dog restrained.
'Your bull's been roaming,' the cop explained.
'Your next-door neighbour has complained.
He's ploughed right through their kale.'

'No, no,' we said, 'That cannot be,
He's over there, beneath that tree,
Peacefully grazing, can't you see?'
Fly flicking with his tail.

Angie noticed on the ground,
His cloven footprints, large and round.
'Look,' she shouted, 'what I've found.
This must be his trail.'

Horrified, her brothers gasped.
Martin chided, 'Girl, you're daft.'
Quietly the bobby laughed.
'Your dad will go to jail!'
He grinned, but she just hid her face
And ran away to find a place
Where she could hide without a trace.
The boys could tell the tale.

Like the rest of us, Dom the dog wasn't as young as he used to be.

So long our dog's been working
Without a thought of shirking
To round all our cattle up.

But passing years brought weariness,
And chronic signs of dreariness,
We need to get a new pup.

So Dom, he's semi-retired now,
And often he's too tired now
To run with a frisky young pup.

In supervisory capacity,
He watches, lest a catastrophe
Should befall an immature pup.

For no one could exaggerate
How a herd of cows exasperate,
An overexcitable pup.

Through all the muck she'd scramble
While Dom, with dignified amble,
Would scorn this stupid young pup.

But now, without hesitation
Or distraction or deviation,
We've a thoroughly well-trained pup.

John had started school. He had been quite a long time at home on his own, so he was really ready to go. Horsington School was in the East Lindsey district of Lincolnshire. I taught in Boston, which was in the Holland area, so our holidays didn't always coincide. It was not long before I had a day off when all the children had to go to school.

I saw them off to their respective schools, and then there was just the two of us left in the house on our own, and I wasn't even pregnant, strange!

Sean went out to do his farm work; I did various chores, and then I decided to cook us a really nice meal and bake some tarts for the children when they came home from school.

As we sat down for lunch, our thoughts went back to our little doll's house with the buttercup curtains at Hobbs Hayes. We had come a long way since then, and Sean had pulled himself up from the orphanage by his bootlaces. Our house was quite comfortable now, although not glamorous by modern standards. As for the farm, how farming has changed since we had got our eighty-year mortgage in Leicestershire! Our little mixed smallholding would be totally unviable now. Sean had built up a modern dairy farm. He would have liked to have upgraded the business sufficiently for us to be able to employ a dairyman, but as we were expanding, wages were going up while farm incomes were plummeting. Recently, we have been running hard to stand still. Now we were stocked to capacity. I had taken a back seat in the farm's development, just doing manual work, which I enjoyed, and keeping the bank manager happy with my teacher's salary.

We had been reminiscing too long. Suddenly our peace was shattered as the first contingent came home from school.

'Is tea ready?'

As I watched the kids demolish the jam tarts, my thoughts reverted to that train journey between East Croyden and London Bridge. I looked at John with his mouth plastered with jam.

'Yes, it was well worth the extra mile for the extra child, who could deny it? One and one make ten!'

EPILOGUE

I was now living in the farmhouse on my own. All eight children remain loyal as they always have been.

They all continued to help with the milking, although what was initially the privilege of working with Daddy became an irksome duty sometimes relieved by the singing of Irish songs to the accompaniment of the milking machines. As teenagers, they were isolated from their friends and social activities, which worried me. I was glad, yet terrified, when at the age of sixteen they could get mopeds and become more independent. The twins were most unlucky in that the driving licence was £2 until their sixteenth birthday, when it went up to £10. They must have been amongst the first in the country to pay the bigger licence fee.

Now all the younger generation have gone their own ways. However, Martin and Maggie's husband, Russell, are still running the farm along with their contracting business. Sean's foresight in putting up a large umbrella building is much appreciated now in the twenty-first century, when farm contracting needs are so different from 1960s dairying.

I am particularly grateful to the pair of them for looking after Sean's suckler herd during his failing health.

As for the house, well, the central heating is run on oil, not straw, but the Rayburn is still in the living room. It is not in use. The chimney has been restored with a plastic pudding basin, and the side of the fire box is paper but with the high mantelshelf over. It keeps the character of the farmhouse. The lads cut my hedge and mow my lawn and do bits of maintenance around the house, and the girls all live near enough for me to call on them any time I need to.

Now I have slightly more financial elbow room, so I can make up for being so tight with the children when they were little.

I am exceptionally lucky in that all my nine grandchildren live within a radius of about twenty-five miles.

All in all, I have learnt more from my children than they have learnt from me. I must have been very narrow and bigoted back in the fifties. Now, I have a broader and hopefully saner outlook on life. And yes, Eileen, the 'fancy wife' and I are still great friends.

Sean lived until September 1997, keeping in touch with the farm at all times, although at the end, all he could do was sign Ministry of Agriculture documents, which I wasn't allowed to sign, fortunately. His last days were as good as they could be. His bed was turned around so that he could see the front field from the bedroom window, which was hired out to Halstead Hall for horses. Martin was very good in those last few weeks. He had to do all the work, but he was longing to make things easier for himself by altering the rails in the yard. Sean thought they were quite adequate, so Martin left them as they were. After Sean died, he took a year to think about moving them before doing so. I must say it has made things a lot easier, but like most men who are very innovative in their younger days, in their older days, 'it is as it was and ever shall be'. He and Maggie's husband, Russell, are now partners running the farm, but things have changed. Sean's first priority was producing good food; now haylage for horses attracts more money, and food has become unimportant because you can fly it in from anywhere in the world in or out of our seasons. Also our acreage was not large enough to support two families. Whereas Martin would like to be a farmer and contractor on the side, I am afraid it is the other way around—firstly a contractor and secondly a farmer. Also as a Swiss visitor pointed out, all our machinery is imported from Europe.

I was at last able to enjoy the farm. I went for a walk every day over the fields with the dog and sometimes into the forest at the back of the farm, which I called my forest. It belonged to the Forestry Commission and was planted chequer, like alternate oak and pine—the pine trees to nurse the oak trees to make them grow up straight. When they took out the conifers and left the deciduous trees, light got through to the undergrowth. One part was a lovely bluebell forest; on the other side, the bluebells were just starting. It was largely stitchwort when I was there.

It was bought by somebody else who put up notices at the entrances 'Trespassers will be prosecuted'. I didn't see these; I went in from the farm, treated it just the same as ever.

But something happened, and the forest reverted to the Forestry Commission again. When I saw a satellite map, it had a green line around it. I asked what this meant and was told 'freedom to roam'. So now I can go in with a clear conscience and, as long as I don't do any damage, go where I want to.

The dog considers it my forest and quite resents other dogs using it.

It used to be farmland. I have an 1888 Ordnance Survey map (twenty-five inch to the mile) up in the hall at the farm, and it had every tree in the hedge row which existed then marked on it. I also had to phone Ordnance Survey to ask what 'RH4feet' meant. It means root to hedge four feet high, which is a convenient height for a man to trim by hand.

Opposite the house there were three ash trees, which Mother used to say represented the Holy Trinity. They were really one tree which had been bent over when the hedge was laid, and two of the branches grew into trees in their own right. They had struck root but died when we bought the field opposite, and Martin decided to have the ditch dug. They had evidently not penetrated deeply enough, but Martin with his contracting is always careful not to cut saplings unless specifically asked by the owner and is responsible for lots of trees around. He has preserved one adjacent ash sapling and will no doubt soon preserve another so we shall have three genuine ash trees again.

I am a widow now, and Peter is still an eligible bachelor. We are still good friends. I see him about once a year when he picks me up from Nuneaton station in order to see his sister, Barbara. But in no way would I want a closer relationship. He, who has a commendation from the Pope for his services to the Church, has grown excessively precise in his maturing years. On the other hand, I have moved away from the Church altogether and got very rough and ready after farm life and bringing up eight children.

Peter trained as a teacher and taught in the school where Eileen became headmistress. Shelagh is also widowed after an idyllic marriage with Alan, who fully recovered from TB.

As for Sean, I may not have been in love when we married, but I grew to love him very much as time went by, and he made a success of farming 132 acres here in Lincolnshire.

CONCLUSION (2013)

I am afraid maturing years have forced me to leave the farm, and I now live in my daughter's double garage, which has been turned into both tasteful and practical living accommodation for me.

She does all my washing and cooks a meal for me almost every day.

I still keep in touch with the farm as my son comes every Tuesday if farm work allows. He now produces Furze Haylage for Horses as now in our affluent society so many folk keep a horse just for the pleasure of riding it. But in the future, I shall keep my mouth shut as regards giving advice. Last year (2012) was very wet, so he couldn't cut the grass to make first-class haylage. I said, 'Why don't you make hay?'

The horses need to balance the succulent rye grass haylage. His partner cut the hay, but when the Monks' Dyke flooded, it all floated away into the forest. The whole crop was lost!

This year (2013), we have had a lot of snow, and I have needed my wellington boots. I wanted help putting them on. A farmer's wife needing help with her wellies! *Not on!* I thought. Two days later I got them on by myself.

I did not write the kernel of this book with the idea of publishing it. In the days when I was partially sighted, I had to learn to touch-type in order to use the computer, and I wrote a page a day for practice. Since then, Audrey has added pages to it and generally made it presentable.

Now I am almost completely blind; I certainly could not manage without Audrey Whelan's invaluable help.

Another lady to whom I owe a lot is Daisy Baker, who wrote *Travels in a Donkey Trap*, published by Coronet. This I listened to courtesy of the R.N.I.B. who recorded it on their audiobook service. Daisy is a woman of my own heart, who loved meditating in the local wood as I did when I lived on the farm.

Here are my final thoughts . . .

THE FOREST IS MY CATHEDRAL

The forest is my Cathedral,
   With countless columns of oak
   Much loved by country folk.
Tall pines make the nave arcade.

Hazels grow in the glade,
   Gothic windows they create,
   Fan vaulting too, they decorate
With pendent catkins of old gold,

As warmer summer days unfold
   The trees reflect the liturgy,
   Green the colour of Trinity,
Pigeons provide the plainsong chant.

Countless songbirds join the choir,
   Descant skylarks on the wing
   Blackbirds, solo anthems sing,
Each with careful chosen perch,

Autumn colours paint my church,
 With copper, bronze, and yellow leaves,
 They gently flutter from the trees.

When winter days are damp and cold,
 Advent's sombre grey and brown
 Await the season's gorgeous crown
When the Christmas babe is born.

With coming of Epiphany
 All is clothed in purest white
 Glistening in the hoar frost light,
And flakes of snow, the New Year greet.

Again in penitential Lent
 Nature's still in slumber deep,
 No warmth to rouse her from her sleep
Then, with longer, lighter days,

Comes the long awaited spring
 With Easter's resurrection theme,
 Nature rises from her dream
And all the forest bursts with life.

I am very happy now, living in a village, especially where the people are so friendly. I was originally a Londoner, and Londoners are noted for keeping themselves to themselves. I very much enjoyed my life on the farm although it was rather isolated. The adjoining village was Stixwould, so folk who came to see us said that we lived 'in the sticks', but now I am older, I enjoy having neighbours.

Lightning Source UK Ltd.
Milton Keynes UK
UKOW04f2353080615

253130UK00001B/59/P